NIST Special Publication 800-30
Revision 1

Guide for Conducting Risk Assessments

NIST
**National Institute of
Standards and Technology**
U.S. Department of Commerce

**JOINT TASK FORCE
TRANSFORMATION INITIATIVE**

INFORMATION SECURITY

Computer Security Division
Information Technology Laboratory
National Institute of Standards and Technology
Gaithersburg, MD 20899-8930

September 2012

U.S. Department of Commerce
Rebecca M. Blank, Acting Secretary

National Institute of Standards and Technology
*Patrick D. Gallagher, Under Secretary for Standards and Technology
and Director*

Reports on Computer Systems Technology

The Information Technology Laboratory (ITL) at the National Institute of Standards and Technology (NIST) promotes the U.S. economy and public welfare by providing technical leadership for the nation's measurement and standards infrastructure. ITL develops tests, test methods, reference data, proof of concept implementations, and technical analyses to advance the development and productive use of information technology. ITL's responsibilities include the development of management, administrative, technical, and physical standards and guidelines for the cost-effective security and privacy of other than national security-related information in federal information systems. The Special Publication 800-series reports on ITL's research, guidelines, and outreach efforts in information system security, and its collaborative activities with industry, government, and academic organizations.

Authority

This publication has been developed by NIST to further its statutory responsibilities under the Federal Information Security Management Act (FISMA), Public Law (P.L.) 107-347. NIST is responsible for developing information security standards and guidelines, including minimum requirements for federal information systems, but such standards and guidelines shall not apply to national security systems without the express approval of appropriate federal officials exercising policy authority over such systems. This guideline is consistent with the requirements of the Office of Management and Budget (OMB) Circular A-130, Section 8b(3), *Securing Agency Information Systems*, as analyzed in Circular A-130, Appendix IV: *Analysis of Key Sections*. Supplemental information is provided in Circular A-130, Appendix III, *Security of Federal Automated Information Resources*.

Nothing in this publication should be taken to contradict the standards and guidelines made mandatory and binding on federal agencies by the Secretary of Commerce under statutory authority. Nor should these guidelines be interpreted as altering or superseding the existing authorities of the Secretary of Commerce, Director of the OMB, or any other federal official. This publication may be used by nongovernmental organizations on a voluntary basis and is not subject to copyright in the United States. Attribution would, however, be appreciated by NIST.

Certain commercial entities, equipment, or materials may be identified in this document in order to describe an experimental procedure or concept adequately. Such identification is not intended to imply recommendation or endorsement by NIST, nor is it intended to imply that the entities, materials, or equipment are necessarily the best available for the purpose.

There may be references in this publication to other publications currently under development by NIST in accordance with its assigned statutory responsibilities. The information in this publication, including concepts and methodologies, may be used by federal agencies even before the completion of such companion publications. Thus, until each publication is completed, current requirements, guidelines, and procedures, where they exist, remain operative. For planning and transition purposes, federal agencies may wish to closely follow the development of these new publications by NIST.

Organizations are encouraged to review all draft publications during public comment periods and provide feedback to NIST. All NIST publications are available at http://csrc.nist.gov/publications.

Compliance with NIST Standards and Guidelines

In accordance with the provisions of FISMA,[1] the Secretary of Commerce shall, on the basis of standards and guidelines developed by NIST, prescribe standards and guidelines pertaining to federal information systems. The Secretary shall make standards compulsory and binding to the extent determined necessary by the Secretary to improve the efficiency of operation or security of federal information systems. Standards prescribed shall include information security standards that provide minimum information security requirements and are otherwise necessary to improve the security of federal information and information systems.

- Federal Information Processing Standards (FIPS) are approved by the Secretary of Commerce and issued by NIST in accordance with FISMA. FIPS are compulsory and binding for federal agencies.[2] FISMA requires that federal agencies comply with these standards, and therefore, agencies may not waive their use.

- Special Publications (SPs) are developed and issued by NIST as recommendations and guidance documents. For other than national security programs and systems, federal agencies must follow those NIST Special Publications mandated in a Federal Information Processing Standard. FIPS 200 mandates the use of Special Publication 800-53, as amended. In addition, OMB policies (including OMB Reporting Instructions for FISMA and Agency Privacy Management) state that for other than national security programs and systems, federal agencies must follow certain specific NIST Special Publications.[3]

- Other security-related publications, including interagency reports (NISTIRs) and ITL Bulletins, provide technical and other information about NIST's activities. These publications are mandatory only when specified by OMB.

- Compliance schedules for NIST security standards and guidelines are established by OMB in policies, directives, or memoranda (e.g., annual FISMA Reporting Guidance).[4]

---

[1] The E-Government Act (P.L. 107-347) recognizes the importance of information security to the economic and national security interests of the United States. Title III of the E-Government Act, entitled the Federal Information Security Management Act (FISMA), emphasizes the need for organizations to develop, document, and implement an organization-wide program to provide security for the information systems that support its operations and assets.

[2] The term *agency* is used in this publication in lieu of the more general term *organization* only in those circumstances where its usage is directly related to other source documents such as federal legislation or policy.

[3] While federal agencies are required to follow certain specific NIST Special Publications in accordance with OMB policy, there is flexibility in how agencies apply the guidance. Federal agencies apply the security concepts and principles articulated in the NIST Special Publications in accordance with and in the context of the agency's missions, business functions, and environment of operation. Consequently, the application of NIST guidance by federal agencies can result in different security solutions that are equally acceptable, compliant with the guidance, and meet the OMB definition of *adequate security* for federal information systems. Given the high priority of information sharing and transparency within the federal government, agencies also consider reciprocity in developing their information security solutions. When assessing federal agency compliance with NIST Special Publications, Inspectors General, evaluators, auditors, and assessors consider the intent of the security concepts and principles articulated within the specific guidance document and how the agency applied the guidance in the context of its mission/business responsibilities, operational environment, and unique organizational conditions.

[4] Unless otherwise stated, all references to NIST publications in this document (i.e., Federal Information Processing Standards and Special Publications) are to the most recent version of the publication.

Acknowledgements

This publication was developed by the *Joint Task Force Transformation Initiative* Interagency Working Group with representatives from the Civil, Defense, and Intelligence Communities in an ongoing effort to produce a unified information security framework for the federal government. The National Institute of Standards and Technology wishes to acknowledge and thank the senior leaders from the Departments of Commerce and Defense, the Office of the Director of National Intelligence, the Committee on National Security Systems, and the members of the interagency technical working group whose dedicated efforts contributed significantly to the publication. The senior leaders, interagency working group members, and their organizational affiliations include:

Department of Defense

Teresa M. Takai
DoD Chief Information Officer

Richard Hale
Deputy Chief Information Officer for Cybersecurity

Paul Grant
Director, Cybersecurity Policy

Dominic Cussatt
Deputy Director, Cybersecurity Policy

Kurt Eleam
Policy Advisor

Office of the Director of National Intelligence

Adolpho Tarasiuk Jr.
Assistant DNI and Intelligence Community Chief Information Officer

Charlene Leubecker
Deputy Intelligence Community Chief Information Officer

Catherine A. Henson
Director, Data Management

Greg Hall
Chief, Risk Management and Information Security Programs Division

National Institute of Standards and Technology

Charles H. Romine
Director, Information Technology Laboratory

Donna Dodson
Cybersecurity Advisor, Information Technology Laboratory

Donna Dodson
Chief, Computer Security Division

Ron Ross
FISMA Implementation Project Leader

Committee on National Security Systems

Teresa M. Takai
Chair, CNSS

Richard Spires
Co-Chair, CNSS

Dominic Cussatt
CNSS Subcommittee Co-Chair

Jeffrey Wilk
CNSS Subcommittee Co-Chair

Joint Task Force Transformation Initiative Interagency Working Group

Ron Ross
NIST, JTF Leader

Deborah Bodeau
The MITRE Corporation

Peter Williams
Booz Allen Hamilton

Gary Stoneburner
Johns Hopkins APL

Steve Rodrigo
Tenacity Solutions, Inc.

Karen Quigg
The MITRE Corporation

Jennifer Fabius
The MITRE Corporation

Peter Gouldmann
Department of State

Christina Sames
TASC

Kelley Dempsey
NIST

Arnold Johnson
NIST

Christian Enloe
NIST

In addition to the above acknowledgments, a special note of thanks goes to Peggy Himes and Elizabeth Lennon of NIST for their superb technical editing and administrative support. The authors also gratefully acknowledge and appreciate the significant contributions from individuals and organizations in the public and private sectors, both nationally and internationally, whose thoughtful and constructive comments improved the overall quality, thoroughness, and usefulness of this publication.

DEVELOPING COMMON INFORMATION SECURITY FOUNDATIONS

COLLABORATION AMONG PUBLIC AND PRIVATE SECTOR ENTITIES

In developing standards and guidelines required by FISMA, NIST consults with other federal agencies and offices as well as the private sector to improve information security, avoid unnecessary and costly duplication of effort, and ensure that NIST publications are complementary with the standards and guidelines employed for the protection of national security systems. In addition to its comprehensive public review and vetting process, NIST is collaborating with the Office of the Director of National Intelligence (ODNI), the Department of Defense (DoD), and the Committee on National Security Systems (CNSS) to establish a common foundation for information security across the federal government. A common foundation for information security will provide the Intelligence, Defense, and Civil sectors of the federal government and their contractors, more uniform and consistent ways to manage the risk to organizational operations and assets, individuals, other organizations, and the Nation that results from the operation and use of information systems. A common foundation for information security will also provide a strong basis for reciprocal acceptance of security authorization decisions and facilitate information sharing. NIST is also working with public and private sector entities to establish specific mappings and relationships between the security standards and guidelines developed by NIST and the International Organization for Standardization and International Electrotechnical Commission (ISO/IEC).

Table of Contents

Prologue

"... Through the process of risk management, leaders must consider risk to U.S. interests from adversaries using cyberspace to their advantage and from our own efforts to employ the global nature of cyberspace to achieve objectives in military, intelligence, and business operations..."

"... For operational plans development, the combination of threats, vulnerabilities, and impacts must be evaluated in order to identify important trends and decide where effort should be applied to eliminate or reduce threat capabilities; eliminate or reduce vulnerabilities; and assess, coordinate, and deconflict all cyberspace operations..."

"... Leaders at all levels are accountable for ensuring readiness and security to the same degree as in any other domain..."

-- THE NATIONAL STRATEGY FOR CYBERSPACE OPERATIONS
   OFFICE OF THE CHAIRMAN, JOINT CHIEFS OF STAFF, U.S. DEPARTMENT OF DEFENSE

CAUTIONARY NOTES

SCOPE AND APPLICABILITY OF RISK ASSESSMENTS

- Risk assessments are a key part of effective risk management and facilitate decision making at all three tiers in the risk management hierarchy including the organization level, mission/business process level, and information system level.

- Because risk management is ongoing, risk assessments are conducted throughout the system development life cycle, from pre-system acquisition (i.e., material solution analysis and technology development), through system acquisition (i.e., engineering/manufacturing development and production/deployment), and on into sustainment (i.e., operations/support).

- There are no specific requirements with regard to: (i) the formality, rigor, or level of detail that characterizes any particular risk assessment; (ii) the methodologies, tools, and techniques used to conduct such risk assessments; or (iii) the format and content of assessment results and any associated reporting mechanisms. Organizations have maximum flexibility on how risk assessments are conducted and are encouraged to apply the guidance in this document so that the various needs of organizations can be addressed and the risk assessment activities can be integrated into broader organizational risk management processes.

- Organizations are also cautioned that risk assessments are often not precise instruments of measurement and reflect: (i) the limitations of the specific assessment methodologies, tools, and techniques employed; (ii) the subjectivity, quality, and trustworthiness of the data used; (iii) the interpretation of assessment results; and (iv) the skills and expertise of those individuals or groups conducting the assessments.

- Since cost, timeliness, and ease of use are a few of the many important factors in the application of risk assessments, organizations should attempt to reduce the level of effort for risk assessments by sharing risk-related information, whenever possible.

CHAPTER ONE

INTRODUCTION

THE NEED FOR RISK ASSESSMENTS TO SUPPORT ENTERPRISE-WIDE RISK MANAGEMENT

Organizations[5] in the public and private sectors depend on information technology[6] and information systems[7] to successfully carry out their missions and business functions. Information systems can include very diverse entities ranging from office networks, financial and personnel systems to very specialized systems (e.g., industrial/process control systems, weapons systems, telecommunications systems, and environmental control systems). Information systems are subject to serious *threats* that can have adverse effects on organizational operations and assets, individuals, other organizations, and the Nation by exploiting both known and unknown *vulnerabilities* to compromise the confidentiality, integrity, or availability of the information being processed, stored, or transmitted by those systems. Threats to information systems can include purposeful attacks, environmental disruptions, human/machine errors, and structural failures, and can result in harm to the national and economic security interests of the United States. Therefore, it is imperative that leaders and managers at all levels understand their responsibilities and are held accountable for managing information security risk—that is, the risk associated with the operation and use of information systems that support the missions and business functions of their organizations.

Risk assessment is one of the fundamental components of an organizational risk management process as described in NIST Special Publication 800-39. Risk assessments are used to identify, estimate, and prioritize risk to organizational operations (i.e., mission, functions, image, and reputation), organizational assets, individuals, other organizations, and the Nation, resulting from the operation and use of information systems. The purpose of risk assessments is to inform decision makers and support risk responses by identifying: (i) relevant threats to organizations or threats directed through organizations against other organizations; (ii) vulnerabilities both internal and external to organizations; (iii) impact (i.e., harm) to organizations that may occur given the potential for threats exploiting vulnerabilities; and (iv) likelihood that harm will occur. The end result is a determination of risk (i.e., typically a function of the degree of harm and likelihood of harm occurring). Risk assessments can be conducted at all three tiers in the risk management hierarchy—including Tier 1 (organization level), Tier 2 (mission/business process level), and Tier 3 (information system level). At Tiers 1 and 2, organizations use risk assessments to evaluate, for example, systemic information security-related risks associated with organizational governance and management activities, mission/business processes, enterprise architecture, or the funding of information security programs. At Tier 3, organizations use risk assessments to more effectively support the implementation of the *Risk Management Framework* (i.e., security categorization; security control selection, implementation, and assessment; information system and common control authorization; and security control monitoring).[8]

---

[5] The term *organization* describes an entity of any size, complexity, or positioning within an organizational structure (e.g., a federal agency or, as appropriate, any of its operational elements) that is charged with carrying out assigned mission/business processes and that uses information systems in support of those processes.

[6] Organizations also manage information technology in the form of common infrastructures, sets of shared services, and sets of common controls.

[7] An *information system* is a discrete set of information resources organized for the collection, processing, maintenance, use, sharing, dissemination, or disposition of information.

[8] The Risk Management Framework is described in NIST Special Publication 800-37.

1.1 PURPOSE AND APPLICABILITY

The purpose of Special Publication 800-30 is to provide guidance for conducting risk assessments of federal information systems and organizations, amplifying the guidance in Special Publication 800-39. Risk assessments, carried out at all three tiers in the risk management hierarchy, are part of an overall risk management process—providing senior leaders/executives with the information needed to determine appropriate courses of action in response to identified risks. In particular, this document provides guidance for carrying out each of the steps in the *risk assessment process* (i.e., preparing for the assessment, conducting the assessment, communicating the results of the assessment, and maintaining the assessment) and how risk assessments and other organizational risk management processes complement and inform each other. Special Publication 800-30 also provides guidance to organizations on identifying specific risk factors to monitor on an ongoing basis, so that organizations can determine whether risks have increased to unacceptable levels (i.e., exceeding organizational risk tolerance) and different courses of action should be taken.

This publication satisfies the requirements of FISMA and meets or exceeds the information security requirements established for executive agencies[9] by the Office of Management and Budget (OMB) in Circular A-130, Appendix III, *Security of Federal Automated Information Resources*. The guidelines in this publication are applicable to all federal information systems other than those systems designated as national security systems as defined in 44 U.S.C., Section 3542. The guidelines have been broadly developed from a technical perspective to complement similar guidelines for national security systems and may be used for such systems with the approval of appropriate federal officials exercising policy authority over such systems. State, local, and tribal governments, as well as private sector organizations are encouraged to consider using these guidelines, as appropriate.

1.2 TARGET AUDIENCE

This publication is intended to serve a diverse group of risk management professionals including:

- Individuals with oversight responsibilities for risk management (e.g., heads of agencies, chief executive officers, chief operating officers, risk executive [function]);

- Individuals with responsibilities for conducting organizational missions/business functions (e.g., mission/business owners, information owners/stewards, authorizing officials);

- Individuals with responsibilities for acquiring information technology products, services, or information systems (e.g., acquisition officials, procurement officers, contracting officers);

- Individuals with information system/security design, development, and implementation responsibilities (e.g., program managers, enterprise architects, information security architects, information system/security engineers, information systems integrators);

- Individuals with information security oversight, management, and operational responsibilities (e.g., chief information officers, senior information security officers,[10] information security managers, information system owners, common control providers); and

---

[9] An *executive agency* is: (i) an executive department specified in 5 U.S.C., Section 101; (ii) a military department specified in 5 U.S.C., Section 102; (iii) an independent establishment as defined in 5 U.S.C., Section 104(1); and (iv) a wholly owned government corporation fully subject to the provisions of 31 U.S.C., Chapter 91. In this publication, the term *executive agency* is synonymous with the term *federal agency*.

[10] At the *agency* level, this position is known as the Senior Agency Information Security Officer. Organizations may also refer to this position as the *Chief Information Security Officer*.

- Individuals with information security/risk assessment and monitoring responsibilities (e.g., system evaluators, penetration testers, security control assessors, risk assessors, independent verifiers/validators, inspectors general, auditors).

1.3 RELATED PUBLICATIONS

The risk assessment approach described in this publication is supported by a series of security standards and guidelines necessary for managing information security risk. In addition to this publication, the Special Publications developed by the Joint Task Force Transformation Initiative supporting the unified information security framework for the federal government include:

- Special Publication 800-39, *Managing Information Security Risk: Organization, Mission, and Information System View*;[11]

- Special Publication 800-37, *Guide for Applying the Risk Management Framework to Federal Information Systems: A Security Life Cycle Approach*;

- Special Publication 800-53, *Recommended Security Controls for Federal Information Systems and Organizations*; and

- Special Publication 800-53A, *Guide for Assessing the Security Controls in Federal Information Systems and Organizations: Building Effective Security Assessment Plans*.

The concepts and principles associated with the risk assessment processes and approaches contained in this publication are intended to be similar to and consistent with the processes and approaches described in International Organization for Standardization (ISO) and International Electrotechnical Commission (IEC) standards. Extending the concepts and principles of these international standards for the federal government and its contractors and promoting the reuse of risk assessment results, reduces the burden on organizations that must conform to ISO/IEC and NIST standards.

1.4 ORGANIZATION OF THIS SPECIAL PUBLICATION

The remainder of this special publication is organized as follows:

- **Chapter Two** describes: (i) the risk management process and how risk assessments are an integral part of that process; (ii) the basic terminology used in conducting risk assessments; and (iii) how risk assessments can be applied across the organization's risk management tiers (i.e., organization level, mission/business process level, and information system level).

- **Chapter Three** describes the process of assessing information security risk including: (i) a high-level overview of the risk assessment process; (ii) the activities necessary to prepare for a risk assessment; (iii) the activities necessary to conduct a risk assessment; (iv) the activities necessary to communicate risk assessment results and share risk-related information across the organization; and (v) the activities necessary to maintain the results of a risk assessment.

- **Supporting appendices** provide additional risk assessment information including: (i) general references; (ii) a glossary of terms; (iii) acronyms; (iv) threat sources; (v) threat events; (vi) vulnerabilities and predisposing conditions; (vii) likelihood of threat event occurrence; (viii) organizational impact; (ix) risk determination; (x) informing risk response; (xi) essential information for risk assessment reports; and (xii) a summary of risk assessment tasks.

---

[11] Special Publication 800-39 supersedes Special Publication 800-30 as the primary source for guidance on information security risk management.

CHAPTER TWO

THE FUNDAMENTALS

BASIC CONCEPTS ASSOCIATED WITH RISK ASSESSMENTS

This chapter describes the fundamental concepts associated with assessing information security risk within an organization including: (i) a high-level overview of the risk management process and the role risk assessments play in that process; (ii) the basic concepts used in conducting risk assessments; and (iii) how risk assessments can be applied across the organization's risk management tiers.[12]

2.1 RISK MANAGEMENT PROCESS

Risk assessment is a key component of a holistic, organization-wide *risk management process* as defined in NIST Special Publication 800-39, *Managing Information Security Risk: Organization, Mission, and Information System View*. Risk management processes include: (i) framing risk; (ii) assessing risk; (iii) responding to risk; and (iv) monitoring risk. Figure 1 illustrates the four steps in the risk management process—including the risk assessment step and the information and communications flows necessary to make the process work effectively.[13]

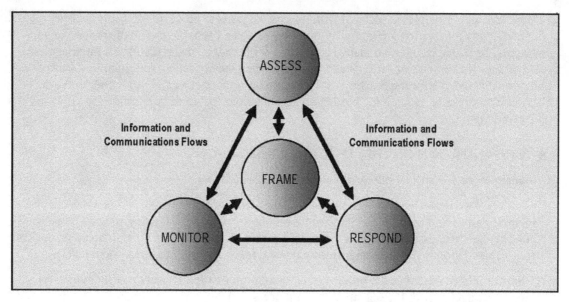

FIGURE 1: RISK ASSESSMENT WITHIN THE RISK MANAGEMENT PROCESS

The first component of risk management addresses how organizations *frame* risk or establish a risk context—that is, describing the environment in which risk-based decisions are made. The purpose of the risk framing component is to produce a *risk management strategy* that addresses how organizations intend to assess risk, respond to risk, and monitor risk—making explicit and

---

[12] NIST Special Publication 800-39 provides guidance on the three tiers in the risk management hierarchy including Tier 1 (organization), Tier 2 (mission/business process), and Tier 3 (information system).

[13] Many of the outputs from the risk framing step provide essential inputs to the risk assessment step and the associated risk assessment process. These include, for example, the risk management strategy, organizational risk tolerance, risk assessment methodology, assumptions, constraints, and mission/business priorities.

transparent the risk perceptions that organizations routinely use in making both investment and operational decisions. The risk management strategy establishes a foundation for managing risk and delineates the boundaries for risk-based decisions within organizations.[14]

The second component of risk management addresses how organizations *assess* risk within the context of the organizational risk frame. The purpose of the risk assessment component is to identify: (i) threats to organizations (i.e., operations, assets, or individuals) or threats directed through organizations against other organizations or the Nation; (ii) vulnerabilities internal and external to organizations;[15] (iii) the harm (i.e., adverse impact) that may occur given the potential for threats exploiting vulnerabilities; and (iv) the likelihood that harm will occur. The end result is a determination of risk (i.e., typically a function of the degree of harm and likelihood of harm occurring).

The third component of risk management addresses how organizations *respond* to risk once that risk is determined based on the results of a risk assessment. The purpose of the risk response component is to provide a consistent, organization-wide response to risk in accordance with the organizational risk frame by: (i) developing alternative courses of action for responding to risk; (ii) evaluating the alternative courses of action; (iii) determining appropriate courses of action consistent with organizational risk tolerance; and (iv) implementing risk responses based on selected courses of action.

The fourth component of risk management addresses how organizations *monitor* risk over time. The purpose of the risk monitoring component is to: (i) determine the ongoing effectiveness of risk responses (consistent with the organizational risk frame); (ii) identify risk-impacting changes to organizational information systems and the environments in which the systems operate;[16] and (iii) verify that planned risk responses are implemented and information security requirements derived from and traceable to organizational missions/business functions, federal legislation, directives, regulations, policies, standards, and guidelines are satisfied.

2.2 RISK ASSESSMENT

This publication focuses on the risk assessment component of risk management—providing a step-by-step process for organizations on: (i) how to prepare for risk assessments; (ii) how to conduct risk assessments; (iii) how to communicate risk assessment results to key organizational personnel; and (iv) how to maintain the risk assessments over time. Risk assessments are not simply one-time activities that provide permanent and definitive information for decision makers to guide and inform responses to information security risks. Rather, organizations employ risk assessments on an ongoing basis throughout the system development life cycle and across all of the tiers in the risk management hierarchy—with the frequency of the risk assessments and the resources applied during the assessments, commensurate with the expressly defined purpose and scope of the assessments.

---

[14] In the absence of an explicit or formal organizational risk management strategy, organizational resources (e.g., tools, data repositories) and references (e.g., exemplary risk assessment reports) can be used to discern those aspects of the organization's approach to risk management that affect risk assessment.

[15] Organizational vulnerabilities are not confined to information systems but can include, for example, vulnerabilities in governance structures, mission/business processes, enterprise architecture, information security architecture, facilities, equipment, system development life cycle processes, supply chain activities, and external service providers.

[16] Environments of operation include, but are not limited to: the threat space; vulnerabilities; missions/business functions; mission/business processes; enterprise and information security architectures; information technologies; personnel; facilities; supply chain relationships; organizational governance/culture; procurement/acquisition processes; organizational policies/procedures; organizational assumptions, constraints, risk tolerance, and priorities/trade-offs).

Risk assessments address the potential adverse impacts to organizational operations and assets, individuals, other organizations, and the economic and national security interests of the United States, arising from the operation and use of information systems and the information processed, stored, and transmitted by those systems. Organizations conduct risk assessments to determine risks that are common to the organization's core missions/business functions, mission/business processes, mission/business segments, common infrastructure/support services, or information systems. Risk assessments can support a wide variety of risk-based decisions and activities by organizational officials across all three tiers in the risk management hierarchy including, but not limited to, the following:

- Development of an information security architecture;

- Definition of interconnection requirements for information systems (including systems supporting mission/business processes and common infrastructure/support services);

- Design of security solutions for information systems and environments of operation including selection of security controls, information technology products, suppliers/supply chain, and contractors;

- Authorization (or denial of authorization) to operate information systems or to use security controls inherited by those systems (i.e., common controls);

- Modification of missions/business functions and/or mission/business processes permanently, or for a specific time frame (e.g., until a newly discovered threat or vulnerability is addressed, until a compensating control is replaced);

- Implementation of security solutions (e.g., whether specific information technology products or configurations for those products meet established requirements); and

- Operation and maintenance of security solutions (e.g., continuous monitoring strategies and programs, ongoing authorizations).

Because organizational missions and business functions, supporting mission/business processes, information systems, threats, and environments of operation tend to change over time, the validity and usefulness of any risk assessment is bounded in time.

2.3 KEY RISK CONCEPTS

Risk is a measure of the extent to which an entity is threatened by a potential circumstance or event, and is typically a function of: (i) the adverse impacts that would arise if the circumstance or event occurs; and (ii) the likelihood of occurrence. Information security risks are those risks that arise from the loss of confidentiality, integrity, or availability of information or information systems and reflect the potential adverse impacts to organizational operations (i.e., mission, functions, image, or reputation), organizational assets, individuals, other organizations, and the Nation. *Risk assessment* is the process of identifying, estimating, and prioritizing information security risks. Assessing risk requires the careful analysis of threat and vulnerability information to determine the extent to which circumstances or events could adversely impact an organization and the likelihood that such circumstances or events will occur.

A *risk assessment methodology* typically includes: (i) a risk assessment process (as described in Chapter Three); (ii) an explicit *risk model*, defining key terms and assessable risk factors and the relationships among the factors; (iii) an *assessment approach* (e.g., quantitative, qualitative, or semi-qualitative), specifying the range of values those risk factors can assume during the risk assessment and how combinations of risk factors are identified/analyzed so that values of those factors can be functionally combined to evaluate risk; and (iv) an *analysis approach* (e.g., threat-oriented, asset/impact-oriented, or vulnerability-oriented), describing how combinations of risk factors are identified/analyzed to ensure adequate coverage of the problem space at a consistent level of detail. Risk assessment methodologies are defined by organizations and are a component of the risk management strategy developed during the risk framing step of the risk management process.[17] Figure 2 illustrates the fundamental components in organizational risk frames and the relationships among those components.

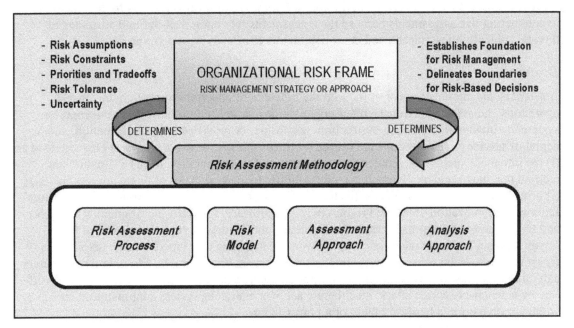

FIGURE 2: RELATIONSHIP AMONG RISK FRAMING COMPONENTS

Organizations can use a single risk assessment methodology or can employ multiple assessment methodologies, with the selection of a specific methodology depending on, for example: (i) the time frame for investment planning or for planning policy changes; (ii) the complexity/maturity of organizational mission/business processes (by enterprise architecture segments); (iii) the phase of the information systems in the system development life cycle; or (iv) the criticality/sensitivity[18] of the information and information systems supporting the core organizational missions/business functions. By making explicit the risk model, the assessment approach, and the analysis approach employed, and requiring as part of the assessment process, a rationale for the assessed values of risk factors, organizations can increase the *reproducibility* and *repeatability* of risk assessments.[19]

---

[17] Risk assessment methodologies are influenced in large measure by the organizational risk management strategy. However, risk assessment methodologies can be customized for each risk assessment based on the purpose and scope of the assessment and the specific inputs organizations choose to make regarding the risk assessment process, risk model, assessment approach, and analysis approach.

[18] NIST Special Publication 800-60 discusses the concepts of *criticality* and *sensitivity* of information with respect to security categorization.

[19] *Reproducibility* refers to the ability of different experts to produce the same results from the same data. *Repeatability* refers to the ability to repeat the assessment in the future, in a manner that is consistent with and hence comparable to prior assessments—enabling the organization to identify trends.

2.3.1 Risk Models

Risk models define the *risk factors* to be assessed and the relationships among those factors.[20] Risk factors are characteristics used in risk models as inputs to determining levels of risk in risk assessments. Risk factors are also used extensively in risk communications to highlight what strongly affects the levels of risk in particular situations, circumstances, or contexts. Typical risk factors include threat, vulnerability, impact, likelihood, and predisposing condition. Risk factors can be decomposed into more detailed characteristics (e.g., threats decomposed into threat sources and threat events).[21] These definitions are important for organizations to document prior to conducting risk assessments because the assessments rely upon well-defined attributes of threats, vulnerabilities, impact, and other risk factors to effectively determine risk.

Threats

A *threat* is any circumstance or event with the potential to adversely impact organizational operations and assets, individuals, other organizations, or the Nation through an information system via unauthorized access, destruction, disclosure, or modification of information, and/or denial of service.[22] Threat events are caused by threat sources. A *threat source* is characterized as: (i) the intent and method targeted at the exploitation of a vulnerability; or (ii) a situation and method that may accidentally exploit a vulnerability. In general, types of threat sources include: (i) hostile cyber or physical attacks; (ii) human errors of omission or commission; (iii) structural failures of organization-controlled resources (e.g., hardware, software, environmental controls); and (iv) natural and man-made disasters, accidents, and failures beyond the control of the organization. Various taxonomies of threat sources have been developed.[23] Some taxonomies of threat sources use the type of adverse impacts as an organizing principle. Multiple threat sources can initiate or cause the same threat event—for example, a provisioning server can be taken off-line by a denial-of-service attack, a deliberate act by a malicious system administrator, an administrative error, a hardware fault, or a power failure.

Risk models differ in the degree of detail and complexity with which threat events are identified. When threat events are identified with great specificity, *threat scenarios* can be modeled, developed, and analyzed.[24] Threat events for cyber or physical attacks are characterized by the tactics, techniques, and procedures (TTPs) employed by adversaries. Understanding adversary-based threat events gives organizations insights into the capabilities associated with certain threat sources. In addition, having greater knowledge about who is carrying out the attacks gives organizations a better understanding of what adversaries desire to gain by the attacks. Knowing

---

[20] Documentation of a risk model includes: (i) identification of risk factors (definitions, descriptions, value scales); and (ii) identification of the relationships among those risk factors (both conceptual relationships, presented descriptively, and algorithms for combining values). The risk model presented in this section (and described in Appendices D-I) does not specify algorithms for combining values.

[21] A risk factor can have a single assessable characteristic (e.g., impact severity) or multiple characteristics, some of which may be assessable and some of which may not be assessable. Characteristics which are not assessable typically help determine what lower-level characteristics are relevant. For example, a threat source has a (characteristic) threat type (using a taxonomy of threat types, which are nominal rather than assessable). The threat type determines which of the more detailed characteristics are relevant (e.g., a threat source of type *adversary* has associated characteristics of capabilities, intent, and targeting, which are directly assessable characteristics).

[22] Organizations can choose to specify threat events as: (i) single events, actions, or circumstances; or (ii) sets and/or sequences of related actions, activities, and/or circumstances.

[23] Appendix D provides an exemplary taxonomy of threat sources and associated threat characteristics.

[24] A *threat scenario* is a set of discrete threat events, attributed to a specific threat source or multiple threat sources, ordered in time, that result in adverse effects.

the intent and targeting aspects of a potential attack helps organizations narrow the set of threat events that are most relevant to consider.

Threat shifting is the response of adversaries to perceived safeguards and/or countermeasures (i.e., security controls), in which adversaries change some characteristic of their intent/targeting in order to avoid and/or overcome those safeguards/countermeasures. Threat shifting can occur in one or more domains including: (i) the time domain (e.g., a delay in an attack or illegal entry to conduct additional surveillance); (ii) the target domain (e.g., selecting a different target that is not as well protected); (iii) the resource domain (e.g., adding resources to the attack in order to reduce uncertainty or overcome safeguards and/or countermeasures); or (iv) the attack planning/attack method domain (e.g., changing the attack weapon or attack path). Threat shifting is a natural consequence of a dynamic set of interactions between threat sources and types of organizational assets targeted. With more sophisticated threat sources, it also tends to default to the path of least resistance to exploit particular vulnerabilities, and the responses are not always predictable. In addition to the safeguards and/or countermeasures implemented and the impact of a successful exploit of an organizational vulnerability, another influence on threat shifting is the benefit to the attacker. That perceived benefit on the attacker side can also influence how much and when threat shifting occurs.

Vulnerabilities and Predisposing Conditions

A *vulnerability* is a weakness in an information system, system security procedures, internal controls, or implementation that could be exploited by a threat source.[25] Most information system vulnerabilities can be associated with security controls that either have not been applied (either intentionally or unintentionally), or have been applied, but retain some weakness. However, it is also important to allow for the possibility of emergent vulnerabilities that can arise naturally over time as organizational missions/business functions evolve, environments of operation change, new technologies proliferate, and new threats emerge. In the context of such change, existing security controls may become inadequate and may need to be reassessed for effectiveness. The tendency for security controls to potentially degrade in effectiveness over time reinforces the need to maintain risk assessments during the entire system development life cycle and also the importance of continuous monitoring programs to obtain ongoing situational awareness of the organizational security posture.

Vulnerabilities are not identified only within information systems. Viewing information systems in a broader context, vulnerabilities can be found in organizational governance structures (e.g., the lack of effective risk management strategies and adequate risk framing, poor intra-agency communications, inconsistent decisions about relative priorities of missions/business functions, or misalignment of enterprise architecture to support mission/business activities). Vulnerabilities can also be found in external relationships (e.g., dependencies on particular energy sources, supply chains, information technologies, and telecommunications providers), mission/business processes (e.g., poorly defined processes or processes that are not risk-aware), and enterprise/information security architectures (e.g., poor architectural decisions resulting in lack of diversity or resiliency in organizational information systems).[26]

---

[25] The *severity* of a vulnerability is an assessment of the relative importance of mitigating/remediating the vulnerability. The severity can be determined by the extent of the potential adverse impact if such a vulnerability is exploited by a threat source. Thus, the severity of vulnerabilities, in general, is context-dependent.

[26] NIST Special Publication 800-39 provides guidance on vulnerabilities at all three tiers in the risk management hierarchy and the potential adverse impact that can occur if threats exploit such vulnerabilities.

In general, risks materialize as a result of a series of threat events, each of which takes advantage of one or more vulnerabilities. Organizations define *threat scenarios* to describe how the events caused by a threat source can contribute to or cause harm. Development of threat scenarios is analytically useful, since some vulnerabilities may not be exposed to exploitation unless and until other vulnerabilities have been exploited. Analysis that illuminates how a set of vulnerabilities, taken together, could be exploited by one or more threat events is therefore more useful than the analysis of individual vulnerabilities. In addition, a threat scenario tells a story, and hence is useful for risk communication as well as for analysis.

In addition to vulnerabilities as described above, organizations also consider predisposing conditions. A *predisposing condition* is a condition that exists within an organization, a mission or business process, enterprise architecture, information system, or environment of operation, which affects (i.e., increases or decreases) the likelihood that threat events, once initiated, result in adverse impacts to organizational operations and assets, individuals, other organizations, or the Nation.[27] Predisposing conditions include, for example, the location of a facility in a hurricane- or flood-prone region (increasing the likelihood of exposure to hurricanes or floods) or a stand-alone information system with no external network connectivity (decreasing the likelihood of exposure to a network-based cyber attack). Vulnerabilities resulting from predisposing conditions that cannot be easily corrected could include, for example, gaps in contingency plans, use of outdated technologies, or weaknesses/deficiencies in information system backup and failover mechanisms. In all cases, these types of vulnerabilities create a predisposition toward threat events having adverse impacts on organizations. Vulnerabilities (including those attributed to predisposing conditions) are part of the overall security posture of organizational information systems and environments of operation that can affect the likelihood of occurrence of a threat event.

Likelihood

The *likelihood of occurrence* is a weighted risk factor based on an analysis of the probability that a given threat is capable of exploiting a given vulnerability (or set of vulnerabilities). The likelihood risk factor combines an estimate of the likelihood that the threat event will be initiated with an estimate of the likelihood of impact (i.e., the likelihood that the threat event results in adverse impacts). For adversarial threats, an assessment of likelihood of occurrence is typically based on: (i) adversary *intent*; (ii) adversary *capability*; and (iii) adversary *targeting*. For other than adversarial threat events, the likelihood of occurrence is estimated using historical evidence, empirical data, or other factors. Note that the likelihood that a threat event will be initiated or will occur is assessed with respect to a specific time frame (e.g., the next six months, the next year, or the period until a specified milestone is reached). If a threat event is almost certain to be initiated or occur in the (specified or implicit) time frame, the risk assessment may take into consideration the estimated frequency of the event. The likelihood of threat occurrence can also be based on the state of the organization (including for example, its core mission/business processes, enterprise architecture, information security architecture, information systems, and environments in which those systems operate)—taking into consideration predisposing conditions and the presence and effectiveness of deployed security controls to protect against unauthorized/undesirable behavior, detect and limit damage, and/or maintain or restore mission/business capabilities. The likelihood of impact addresses the probability (or possibility) that the threat event will result in an adverse impact, regardless of the magnitude of harm that can be expected.

---

[27] The concept of predisposing condition is also related to the term *susceptibility* or *exposure*. Organizations are not susceptible to risk (or exposed to risk) if a threat cannot exploit a vulnerability to cause adverse impact. For example, organizations that do not employ database management systems are not vulnerable to the threat of SQL injections and therefore, are not susceptible to such risk.

Organizations typically employ a three-step process to determine the overall likelihood of threat events. First, organizations assess the likelihood that threat events will be initiated (for adversarial threat events) or will occur (for non-adversarial threat events). Second, organizations assess the likelihood that the threat events once initiated or occurring, will result in adverse impacts or harm to organizational operations and assets, individuals, other organizations, or the Nation. Finally, organizations assess the overall likelihood as a combination of likelihood of initiation/occurrence and likelihood of resulting in adverse impact.

Threat-vulnerability pairing (i.e., establishing a one-to-one relationship between threats and vulnerabilities) may be undesirable when assessing likelihood at the mission/business function level, and in many cases, can be problematic even at the information system level due to the potentially large number of threats and vulnerabilities. This approach typically drives the level of detail in identifying threat events and vulnerabilities, rather than allowing organizations to make effective use of threat information and/or to identify threats at a level of detail that is meaningful. Depending on the level of detail in threat specification, a given threat event could exploit multiple vulnerabilities. In assessing likelihoods, organizations examine vulnerabilities that threat events could exploit and also the mission/business function susceptibility to events for which no security controls or viable implementations of security controls exist (e.g., due to functional dependencies, particularly external dependencies). In certain situations, the most effective way to reduce mission/business risk attributable to information security risk is to redesign the mission/business processes so there are viable work-arounds when information systems are compromised. Using the concept of threat scenarios described above, may help organizations overcome some of the limitations of threat-vulnerability pairing.

Impact

The level of *impact* from a threat event is the magnitude of harm that can be expected to result from the consequences of unauthorized disclosure of information, unauthorized modification of information, unauthorized destruction of information, or loss of information or information system availability. Such harm can be experienced by a variety of organizational and non-organizational stakeholders including, for example, heads of agencies, mission and business owners, information owners/stewards, mission/business process owners, information system owners, or individuals/groups in the public or private sectors relying on the organization—in essence, anyone with a vested interest in the organization's operations, assets, or individuals, including other organizations in partnership with the organization, or the Nation.[28] Organizations make explicit: (i) the process used to conduct impact determinations; (ii) assumptions related to impact determinations; (iii) sources and methods for obtaining impact information; and (iv) the rationale for conclusions reached with regard to impact determinations.

Organizations may explicitly define how established priorities and values guide the identification of high-value assets and the potential adverse impacts to organizational stakeholders. If such information is not defined, priorities and values related to identifying targets of threat sources and associated organizational impacts can typically be derived from strategic planning and policies. For example, security categorization levels indicate the organizational impacts of compromising different types of information. Privacy Impact Assessments and criticality levels (when defined as part of contingency planning or Mission/Business Impact Analysis) indicate the adverse impacts of destruction, corruption, or loss of accountability for information resources to organizations.

---

[28] The term *organizational assets* can have a very wide scope of applicability to include, for example, high-impact programs, physical plant, mission-critical information systems, personnel, equipment, or a logically related group of systems. More broadly, organizational assets represent any resource or set of resources which the organization values, including intangible assets such as image or reputation.

Strategic plans and policies also assert or imply the relative priorities of immediate or near-term mission/business function accomplishment and long-term organizational viability (which can be undermined by the loss of reputation or by sanctions resulting from the compromise of sensitive information). Organizations can also consider the range of effects of threat events including the relative size of the set of resources affected, when making final impact determinations. Risk tolerance assumptions may state that threat events with an impact below a specific value do not warrant further analysis.

Risk

Figure 3 illustrates an example of a risk model including the key risk factors discussed above and the relationship among the factors. Each of the risk factors is used in the risk assessment process in Chapter Three.

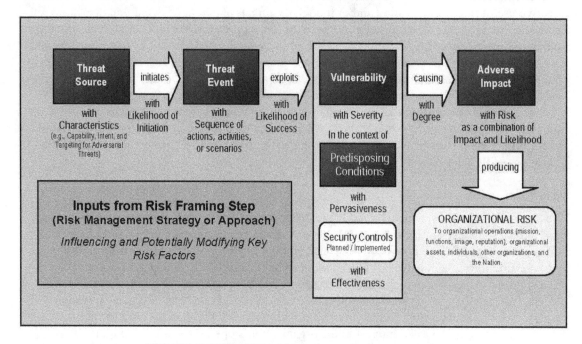

FIGURE 3: GENERIC RISK MODEL WITH KEY RISK FACTORS

As noted above, *risk* is a function of the likelihood of a threat event's occurrence and potential adverse impact should the event occur. This definition accommodates many types of adverse impacts at all tiers in the risk management hierarchy described in Special Publication 800-39 (e.g., damage to image or reputation of the organization or financial loss at Tier 1; inability to successfully execute a specific mission/business process at Tier 2; or the resources expended in responding to an information system incident at Tier 3). It also accommodates relationships among impacts (e.g., loss of current or future mission/business effectiveness due to the loss of data confidentiality; loss of confidence in critical information due to loss of data or system integrity; or unavailability or degradation of information or information systems). This broad definition also allows risk to be represented as a single value or as a vector (i.e., multiple values), in which different types of impacts are assessed separately. For purposes of risk communication, risk is generally grouped according to the types of adverse impacts (and possibly the time frames in which those impacts are likely to be experienced).

Aggregation

Organizations may use risk *aggregation* to roll up several discrete or lower-level risks into a more general or higher-level risk. Organizations may also use risk aggregation to efficiently manage the scope and scale of risk assessments involving multiple information systems and multiple mission/business processes with specified relationships and dependencies among those systems and processes. Risk aggregation, conducted primarily at Tiers 1 and 2 and occasionally at Tier 3, assesses the overall risk to organizational operations, assets, and individuals given the set of discrete risks. In general, for discrete risks (e.g., the risk associated with a single information system supporting a well-defined mission/business process), the worst-case impact establishes an upper bound for the overall risk to organizational operations, assets, and individuals.[29] One issue for risk aggregation is that this upper bound for risk may fail to apply. For example, it may be advantageous for organizations to assess risk at the organization level when multiple risks materialize concurrently or when the same risk materializes repeatedly over a period of time. In such situations, there is the possibility that the amount of overall risk incurred is beyond the risk capacity of the organization, and therefore the overall impact to organizational operations and assets (i.e., mission/business impact) goes beyond that which was originally assessed for each specific risk.

When aggregating risk, organizations consider the relationship among various discrete risks. For example, there may be a cause and effect relationship in that if one risk materializes, another risk is more or less likely to materialize. If there is a direct or inverse relationship among discrete risks, then the risks can be coupled (in a qualitative sense) or correlated (in a quantitative sense) either in a positive or negative manner. Risk coupling or correlation (i.e., finding relationships among risks that increase or decrease the likelihood of any specific risk materializing) can be done at Tiers 1, 2, or 3.

Uncertainty

Uncertainty is inherent in the evaluation of risk, due to such considerations as: (i) limitations on the extent to which the future will resemble the past; (ii) imperfect or incomplete knowledge of the threat (e.g., characteristics of adversaries including tactics, techniques, and procedures); (iii) undiscovered vulnerabilities in technologies or products; and (iv) unrecognized dependencies, which can lead to unforeseen impacts. Uncertainty about the value of specific risk factors can also be due to the step in the RMF or phase in the system development life cycle at which a risk assessment is performed. For example, at early phases in the system development life cycle, the presence and effectiveness of security controls may be unknown, while at later phases in the life cycle, the cost of evaluating control effectiveness may outweigh the benefits in terms of more fully informed decision making. Finally, uncertainty can be due to incomplete knowledge of the risks associated with other information systems, mission/ business processes, services, common infrastructures, and/or organizations. The degree of uncertainty in risk assessment results, due to these different reasons, can be communicated in the form of the results (e.g., by expressing results qualitatively, by providing ranges of values rather than single values for identified risks, or by using a visual representations of fuzzy regions rather than points).

---

[29] Security categorizations conducted in accordance with FIPS Publication 199 provide examples of *worst-case* impact analyses (using the high water mark concept). This type of impact analysis provides an upper bound for risk when applied to discrete situations within organizations.

2.3.2 Assessment Approaches

Risk, and its contributing factors, can be assessed in a variety of ways, including quantitatively, qualitatively, or semi-quantitatively. Each risk assessment approach considered by organizations has advantages and disadvantages. A preferred approach (or situation-specific set of approaches) can be selected based on organizational culture and, in particular, attitudes toward the concepts of uncertainty and risk communication. *Quantitative* assessments typically employ a set of methods, principles, or rules for assessing risk based on the use of numbers—where the meanings and proportionality of values are maintained inside and outside the context of the assessment. This type of assessment most effectively supports cost-benefit analyses of alternative risk responses or courses of action. However, the meaning of the quantitative results may not always be clear and may require interpretation and explanation—particularly to explain the assumptions and constraints on using the results. For example, organizations may typically ask if the numbers or results obtained in the risk assessments are reliable or if the differences in the obtained values are meaningful or insignificant. Additionally, the rigor of quantification is significantly lessened when subjective determinations are buried within the quantitative assessments, or when significant uncertainty surrounds the determination of values. The benefits of quantitative assessments (in terms of the rigor, repeatability, and reproducibility of assessment results) can, in some cases, be outweighed by the costs (in terms of the expert time and effort and the possible deployment and use of tools required to make such assessments).

In contrast to quantitative assessments, *qualitative* assessments typically employ a set of methods, principles, or rules for assessing risk based on nonnumerical categories or levels (e.g., very low, low, moderate, high, very high). This type of assessment supports communicating risk results to decision makers. However, the range of values in qualitative assessments is comparatively small in most cases, making the relative prioritization or comparison within the set of reported risks difficult. Additionally, unless each value is very clearly defined or is characterized by meaningful examples, different experts relying on their individual experiences could produce significantly different assessment results. The repeatability and reproducibility of qualitative assessments are increased by the annotation of assessed values (e.g., this value is high because of the following reasons) and by the use of tables or other well-defined functions to combine qualitative values.

Finally, *semi-quantitative* assessments typically employ a set of methods, principles, or rules for assessing risk that uses bins, scales, or representative numbers whose values and meanings are not maintained in other contexts. This type of assessment can provide the benefits of quantitative and qualitative assessments. The bins (e.g., 0-15, 16-35, 36-70, 71-85, 86-100) or scales (e.g., 1-10) translate easily into qualitative terms that support risk communications for decision makers (e.g., a score of 95 can be interpreted as very high), while also allowing relative comparisons between values in different bins or even within the same bin (e.g., the difference between risks scored 70 and 71 respectively is relatively insignificant, while the difference between risks scored 36 and 70 is relatively significant). The role of expert judgment in assigning values is more evident than in a purely quantitative approach. Moreover, if the scales or sets of bins provide sufficient granularity, relative prioritization among results is better supported than in a purely qualitative approach. As in a quantitative approach, rigor is significantly lessened when subjective determinations are buried within assessments, or when significant uncertainty surrounds a determination of value. As with the nonnumeric categories or levels used in a well-founded qualitative approach, each bin or range of values needs to be clearly defined and/or characterized by meaningful examples.

Independent of the type of value scale selected, assessments make explicit the *temporal* element of risk factors. For example, organizations can associate a specific time period with assessments of likelihood of occurrence and assessments of impact severity.

2.3.3 Analysis Approaches

Analysis approaches differ with respect to the orientation or starting point of the risk assessment, level of detail in the assessment, and how risks due to similar threat scenarios are treated. An analysis approach can be: (i) *threat-oriented*; (ii) *asset/impact-oriented*; or (iii) *vulnerability-oriented*.[30] A threat-oriented approach starts with the identification of threat sources and threat events, and focuses on the development of threat scenarios; vulnerabilities are identified in the context of threats, and for adversarial threats, impacts are identified based on adversary intent. An asset/impact-oriented approach starts with the identification of impacts or consequences of concern and critical assets, possibly using the results of a mission or business impact analyses[31] and identifying threat events that could lead to and/or threat sources that could seek those impacts or consequences. A vulnerability-oriented approach starts with a set of predisposing conditions or exploitable weaknesses/deficiencies in organizational information systems or the environments in which the systems operate, and identifies threat events that could exercise those vulnerabilities together with possible consequences of vulnerabilities being exercised. Each analysis approach takes into consideration the same risk factors, and thus entails the same set of risk assessment activities, albeit in different order. Differences in the starting point of the risk assessment can potentially bias the results, causing some risks not to be identified. Therefore, identification of risks from a second orientation (e.g., complementing a threat-oriented analysis approach with an asset/impact-oriented analysis approach) can improve the rigor and effectiveness of the analysis.

In addition to the orientation of the analysis approach, organizations can apply more rigorous analysis techniques (e.g., graph-based analyses) to provide an effective way to account for the many-to-many relationships between: (i) threat sources and threat events (i.e., a single threat event can be caused by multiple threat sources and a single threat source can cause multiple threat events); (ii) threat events and vulnerabilities (i.e., a single threat event can exploit multiple vulnerabilities and a single vulnerability can be exploited by multiple threat events); and (iii) threat events and impacts/assets (i.e., a single threat event can affect multiple assets or have multiple impacts, and a single asset can be affected by multiple threat events).[32] Rigorous analysis approaches also provide a way to account for whether, in the time frame for which risks are assessed, a specific adverse impact could occur (or a specific asset could be harmed) at most once, or perhaps repeatedly, depending on the nature of the impacts and on how organizations (including mission/business processes or information systems) recover from such adverse impacts.

---

[30] Organizations have great flexibility in choosing a particular analysis approach. The specific approach taken is driven by different organizational considerations (e.g., the quality and quantity of information available with respect to threats, vulnerabilities, and impacts/assets; the specific orientation carrying the highest priority for organizations; availability of analysis tools emphasizing certain orientations; or a combination of the above).

[31] A *Business Impact Analysis* (BIA) identifies high-value assets and adverse impacts with respect to the loss of integrity or availability. DHS Federal Continuity Directive 2 provides guidance on BIAs at the organization and mission/business process levels of the risk management hierarchy, respectively. NIST Special Publication 800-34 provides guidance on BIAs at the information system level of the risk management hierarchy.

[32] For example, graph-based analysis techniques (e.g., functional dependency network analysis, attack tree analysis for adversarial threats, fault tree analysis for other types of threats) provide ways to use specific threat events to generate threat scenarios. Graph-based analysis techniques can also provide ways to account for situations in which one event can change the likelihood of occurrence for another event. Attack and fault tree analyses, in particular, can generate multiple threat scenarios that are nearly alike, for purposes of determining the levels of risk. With automated modeling and simulation, large numbers of threat scenarios (e.g., attack/fault trees, traversals of functional dependency networks) can be generated. Thus, graph-based analysis techniques include ways to restrict the analysis to define a reasonable subset of all possible threat scenarios.

2.3.4 Effects of Organizational Culture on Risk Assessments

Organizations can differ in the risk models, assessment approaches, and analysis approaches that they prefer for a variety of reasons. For example, cultural issues[33] can predispose organizations to employ risk models that assume a constant value for one or more possible risk factors, so that some factors that are present in other organizations' models are not represented. Culture can also predispose organizations to employ risk models that require detailed analyses using quantitative assessments (e.g., nuclear safety). Alternately, organizations may prefer qualitative or semi-quantitative assessment approaches. In addition to differences among organizations, differences can also exist within organizations. For example, organizations can use coarse or high-level risk models early in the system development life cycle to select security controls, and subsequently, more detailed models to assess risk to given missions or business functions. Organizational risk frames[34] determine which risk models, assessment approaches, and analysis approaches to use under varying circumstances.

THE USE OF RISK MODELS

A single risk model (consisting of a fixed set of factors, a fixed assessment scale for each factor, and a fixed algorithm for combining factors) cannot meet the diverse needs of the organizations in the public and private sectors that rely on Special Publication 800-30. For example, while some organizations may emphasize adversarial threats and provide detailed information about such threats, other organizations may choose instead to focus on non-adversarial threats, providing greater detail for those types of threats and lesser detail for adversarial threats. Therefore, the risk models developed by organizations with different assumptions regarding threats will involve different factors as well as different levels of detail.

Similarly, within a single organization or community of interest, different assessment scales may be appropriate for different missions/business functions, different categories of information systems, and/or for systems at different stages in the system development life cycle. For example, during an initial risk assessment performed when an information system is first being considered, the information available about threats and vulnerabilities may be nonspecific and highly uncertain. For such risk assessments, a qualitative assessment, using only a few factors, may be appropriate. By contrast, a risk assessment informed by a security controls assessment can be far more specific, and estimates can be made with greater fidelity. For such assessments, a semi-quantitative assessment using the 0-100 value scales may be more appropriate.

The expectation set forth in Special Publications 800-39 and 800-30 is that each organization or community will define a risk model appropriate to its view of risk (i.e., formulas that reflect organizational or community views of which risk factors must be considered, which factors can be combined, which factors must be further decomposed, and how assessed values should be combined algorithmically). Special Publication 800-30 does identify risk factors that are common across a wide spectrum of risk models. In addition, by defining multiple aligned value scales, this publication provides a foundation for a consistent approach to estimating information security risk across the system development life cycle, without forcing assessments early in the life cycle to be more detailed than can be justified by available information.

---

[33] NIST Special Publication 800-39 describes how organizational culture affects risk management.

[34] NIST Special Publication 800-39 defines an organization's risk frame as the set of assumptions, constraints, risk tolerances, priorities, and trade-offs that underpin the organization's risk management strategy—establishing a solid foundation for managing risk and bounding its risk-based decisions.

2.4 APPLICATION OF RISK ASSESSMENTS

As stated previously, risk assessments can be conducted at all three tiers in the risk management hierarchy—*organization level, mission/business process level,* and *information system level.* Figure 4 illustrates the risk management hierarchy defined in NIST Special Publication 800-39, which provides multiple risk perspectives from the strategic level to the tactical level. Traditional risk assessments generally focus at the Tier 3 level (i.e., information system level) and as a result, tend to overlook other significant risk factors that may be more appropriately assessed at the Tier 1 or Tier 2 levels (e.g., exposure of a core mission/business function to an adversarial threat based on information system interconnections).

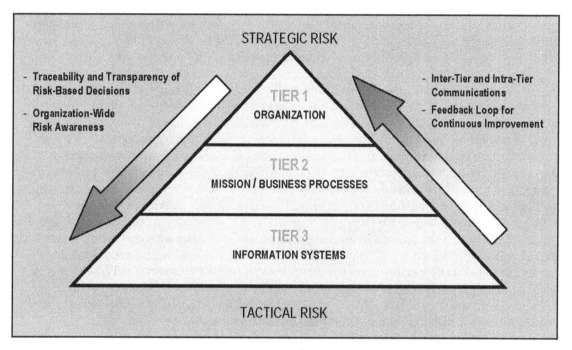

FIGURE 4: RISK MANAGEMENT HIERARCHY

Risk assessments support risk response decisions at the different tiers of the risk management hierarchy. At Tier 1, risk assessments can affect, for example: (i) organization-wide information security programs, policies, procedures, and guidance; (ii) the types of appropriate risk responses (i.e., risk acceptance, avoidance, mitigation, sharing, or transfer); (iii) investment decisions for information technologies/systems; (iv) procurements; (v) minimum organization-wide security controls; (vi) conformance to enterprise/security architectures; and (vii) monitoring strategies and ongoing authorizations of information systems and common controls. At Tier 2, risk assessments can affect, for example: (i) enterprise architecture/security architecture design decisions; (ii) the selection of common controls; (iii) the selection of suppliers, services, and contractors to support organizational missions/business functions; (iv) the development of risk-aware mission/business processes; and (v) the interpretation of information security policies with respect to organizational information systems and environments in which those systems operate. Finally, at Tier 3, risk assessments can affect, for example: (i) design decisions (including the selection, tailoring, and supplementation of security controls and the selection of information technology products for organizational information systems); (ii) implementation decisions (including whether specific information technology products or product configurations meet security control requirements); and (iii) operational decisions (including the requisite level of monitoring activity, the frequency of ongoing information system authorizations, and system maintenance decisions).

Risk assessments can also inform other risk management activities across the three tiers that are not security-related. For example, at Tier 1, risk assessments can provide useful inputs to: (i) operational risk determinations (including business continuity for organizational missions and business functions); (ii) organizational risk determinations (including financial risk, compliance risk, regulatory risk, reputation risk, and cumulative acquisition risk across large-scale projects); and (iii) multiple-impact risk (including supply chain risk and risk involving partnerships). At Tier 2, risk assessments can provide the same useful inputs to operational, organizational, and multiple-impact risks, specific to mission/business processes. At Tier 3, risk assessments can inform assessments of cost, schedule, and performance risks associated with information systems, with information security experts coordinating with program managers, information system owners, and authorizing officials. This type of coordination is essential within organizations in order to eliminate silos and/or stove-piped activities that produce less than optimal or inefficient information technology and security solutions—thus affecting the ability of organizations to carry out assigned missions/business functions with maximum efficiency and cost-effectiveness.

It is important to note that information security risk contributes to non-security risks at each tier. Thus, the results of a risk assessment at a given tier serve as inputs to, and are aligned with, non-security risk management activities at that tier.[35] In addition, the results of risk assessments at lower tiers serve as inputs to risk assessments at higher tiers. Risks can arise on different time scales (e.g., the disclosure of information about current organizational operations can compromise the effectiveness of those operations immediately, while the disclosure of strategic planning information can compromise future operational capabilities). Risk response decisions can also take effect in different time frames (e.g., changes in organizational policies or investment strategies can sometimes require years to take effect, while configuration changes in an individual system can often be implemented immediately). In general, the risk management process tends to move more slowly at Tiers 1 and 2 than at Tier 3. This is due to how organizations typically respond to risks that potentially affect widespread organizational operations and assets—where such risk responses may need to address systemic or institutional issues. However, some Tier 1 decisions (e.g., newly discovered threats or vulnerabilities requiring the implementation of an organization-wide mandate for mitigation) can involve immediate action.

2.4.1 Risk Assessments at the Organizational Tier

At Tier 1, risk assessments support organizational strategies, policies, guidance, and processes for managing risk. Risk assessments conducted at Tier 1 focus on organizational operations, assets, and individuals—comprehensive assessments across mission/business lines. For example, Tier 1 risk assessments may address: (i) the specific types of threats directed at organizations that may be different from other organizations and how those threats affect policy decisions; (ii) systemic weaknesses or deficiencies discovered in multiple organizational information systems capable of being exploited by adversaries; (iii) the potential adverse impact on organizations from the loss or compromise of organizational information (either intentionally or unintentionally); and (iv) the use of new information and computing technologies such as mobile and cloud and the potential effect on the ability of organizations to successfully carry out their missions/business operations while using those technologies. Organization-wide assessments of risk can be based solely on the assumptions, constraints, risk tolerances, priorities, and trade-offs established in the risk framing step (i.e., derived primarily from Tier 1 activities). However, more realistic and meaningful risk assessments are based on assessments conducted across multiple mission/business lines (i.e., derived primarily from Tier 2 activities). The ability of organizations to effectively use Tier 2 risk

---

[35] In particular, risk assessment results support investment risk management. NIST Special Publication 800-65 provides guidance on integrating information security into the Capital Planning and Investment Control (CPIC) process.

assessments as inputs to Tier 1 risk assessments is shaped by such considerations as: (i) the similarity of organizational missions/business functions and mission/business processes; and (ii) the degree of autonomy that organizational entities or subcomponents have with respect to parent organizations. In decentralized organizations or organizations with varied missions/business functions and/or environments of operation, expert analysis may be needed to normalize the results from Tier 2 risk assessments. Finally, risk assessments at Tier 1 take into consideration the identification of mission-essential functions from Continuity of Operations Plans (COOP)[36] prepared by organizations when determining the contribution of Tier 2 risks. Risk assessment results at Tier 1 are communicated to organizational entities at Tier 2 and Tier 3.

2.4.2   Risk Assessments at the Mission/Business Process Tier

At Tier 2, risk assessments support the determination of mission/business process protection and resiliency requirements, and the allocation of those requirements to the enterprise architecture as part of mission/business segments (that support mission/business processes). This allocation is accomplished through an information security architecture embedded within the enterprise architecture. Tier 2 risk assessments also inform and guide decisions on whether, how, and when to use information systems for specific mission/business processes, in particular for alternative mission/business processing in the face of compromised information systems. Risk management and associated risk assessment activities at Tier 2 are closely aligned with the development of Business Continuity Plans (BCPs). Tier 2 risk assessments focus on mission/business segments, which typically include multiple information systems, with varying degrees of criticality and/or sensitivity with regard to core organizational missions/business functions.[37] Risk assessments at Tier 2 can also focus on information security architecture as a critical component of enterprise architecture to help organizations select common controls inherited by organizational information systems at Tier 3. Risk assessment results produced at Tier 2 are communicated to and shared with organizational entities at Tier 3 to help inform and guide the allocation of security controls to information systems and environments in which those systems operate. Tier 2 risk assessments also provide assessments of the security and risk posture of organizational mission/business processes, which inform assessments of organizational risks at Tier 1. Thus, risk assessment results at Tier 2 are routinely communicated to organizational entities at Tier 1 and Tier 3.

2.4.3   Risk Assessments at the Information System Tier

The Tier 2 context and the system development life cycle determine the purpose and define the scope of risk assessment activities at Tier 3. While initial risk assessments (i.e., risk assessments performed for the first time, rather than updating prior risk assessments) can be performed at any phase in the system development life cycle, ideally these assessments should be performed in the Initiation phase.[38] In the Initiation phase, risk assessments evaluate the anticipated vulnerabilities and predisposing conditions affecting the confidentiality, integrity, and availability of information systems in the context of the planned environments of operation. Such assessments inform risk response, enabling information system owners/program managers, together with mission/business owners to make the final decisions about the security controls necessary based on the security categorization and the environment of operation. Risk assessments are also conducted at later phases in the system development life cycle, updating risk assessment results from earlier phases. These risk assessment results for as-built or as-deployed information systems typically include

---

[36] NIST Special Publication 800-34 provides guidance on Information System Contingency Planning (ISCP).

[37] The criticality of information systems to organizational missions/business functions may be identified in Business Impact Analyses.

[38] NIST Special Publication 800-64 provides guidance for security considerations in the system development life cycle.

descriptions of vulnerabilities in the systems, an assessment of the risks associated with each vulnerability (thereby updating the assessment of vulnerability severity), and corrective actions that can be taken to mitigate the risks. The risk assessment results also include an assessment of the overall risk to the organization and the information contained in the information systems by operating the systems as evaluated. Risk assessment results at Tier 3 are communicated to organizational entities at Tier 1 and Tier 2.

Risk assessment activities can be integrated with the steps in the Risk Management Framework (RMF), as defined in NIST Special Publication 800-37. The RMF, in its system development life cycle approach, operates primarily at Tier 3 with some application at Tiers 1 and 2, for example, in the selection of common controls. Risk assessments can be tailored to each step in the RMF as reflected in the purpose and scope of the assessments described in Section 3.1. Risk assessments can also help determine the type of security assessments conducted during various phases of the system development life cycle, the frequency of such assessments, the level of rigor applied during the assessments, the assessment methods used, and the types/number of objects assessed. The benefit of risk assessments conducted as part of the RMF can be realized from both initial assessments and from updated assessments, as described below.

RMF Step 1 – Categorize

Organizations can use initial risk assessments to make security categorization decisions consistent with the risk management strategy provided by the risk executive (function) and as a preparatory step to security control selection. Conducting initial risk assessments brings together the available information on threat sources, threat events, vulnerabilities, and predisposing conditions—thus enabling organizations to use such information to categorize information and information systems based on known and potential threats to and vulnerabilities in organizational information systems and environments in which those systems operate.[39] Security categorization decisions inform the selection of initial baseline security controls. Baseline security controls serve as the starting point for organizational tailoring and supplementation activities described in the RMF Select step.

RMF Step 2 – Select

Organizations can use risk assessments to inform and guide the selection of security controls for organizational information systems and environments of operation. After the initial security control baseline is selected based on the security categorization process, the risk assessment results help organizations: (i) apply appropriate tailoring guidance to adjust the controls based on specific mission/business requirements, assumptions, constraints, priorities, trade-offs, or other organization-defined conditions; and (ii) supplement the controls based on specific and credible threat information.[40] Threat data from risk assessments provide critical information on adversary capabilities, intent, and targeting that may affect the decisions by organizations regarding the selection of additional security controls including the associated costs and benefits. Organizations also consider risk assessment results when selecting common controls (typically a Tier 1 and Tier 2 activity). Risk is introduced if the implementation of a common control results in a single point of failure because the control provides a security capability potentially inherited by multiple information systems. As risk assessments are updated and refined, organizations use the results to modify current security control selections based on the most recent threat and vulnerability information available.

---

[39] Even when an initial risk assessment is performed prior to the existence of an information system, vulnerabilities may be present in certain technologies that will be used in the system, in common controls that will be inherited by the system, or in the environment in which the system will operate.

[40] Supplementation will be incorporated into the tailoring process in NIST Special Publication 800-53, Revision 4.

RMF Step 3 – Implement

Organizations can use risk assessment results to identify alternative implementations of selected security controls (e.g., considering vulnerabilities inherent in one security control implementation versus another). Some information technology products, system components, or architectural configurations may be more susceptible to certain types of threat sources; these susceptibilities are subsequently addressed during security control development and implementation. In addition, the strength of security mechanisms selected for implementation can take into consideration the threat data from risk assessments. Individual configuration settings for information technology products and system components can eliminate vulnerabilities identified during the analysis of threat events. Risk assessment results also help inform decisions regarding the cost, benefit, and risk trade-offs in using one type of technology versus another or how security controls are effectively implemented in particular operational environments (e.g., when compensating controls must be used due to the unavailability of certain technologies). As risk assessments are updated and refined, organizations use the results to help determine if current security control implementations remain effective given changes to the threat space.

RMF Step 4 – Assess

Organizations can use the results from security control assessments to inform risk assessments. Security control assessments (documented in security assessment reports) identify vulnerabilities in organizational information systems and the environments in which those systems operate. Partial or complete failure of deployed security controls or the absence of planned controls represents potential vulnerabilities that can be exploited by threat sources. Organizations use the results from risk assessments to help determine the severity of such vulnerabilities which in turn, can guide and inform organizational risk responses (e.g., prioritizing risk response activities, establishing milestones for corrective actions).

RMF Step 5 – Authorize

Organizations can use risk assessment results to provide risk-related information to authorizing officials. The risk responses carried out by organizations based on the risk assessments result in a known security posture of organizational information systems and environments of operation. Risk assessment results provide essential information to enable authorizing officials to make risk-based decisions on whether to operate those systems in the current security posture or take actions to provide additional security controls, thereby further reducing risk to organizational operations and assets, individuals, other organizations, or the Nation.

RMF Step 6 – Monitor

Organizations can update risk assessments on an ongoing basis using security-related information from organizational continuous monitoring processes.[41] Continuous monitoring processes evaluate: (i) the *effectiveness* of security controls; (ii) *changes* to information systems and environments of operation; and (iii) *compliance* to federal legislation, regulations, directives, policies, standards, and guidance. As risk assessments are updated and refined, organizations use the results to update the risk management strategy, thereby incorporating lessons learned into risk management processes, improving responses to risk, and building a solid foundation of threat and vulnerability information tailored to organizational missions/business functions.

---

[41] NIST Special Publication 800-137 provides guidance on information security continuous monitoring for information systems and organizations.

2.4.4   Risk Communications and Information Sharing

The risk assessment process entails ongoing communications and information sharing among stakeholders to ensure that: (i) the inputs to such assessments are as accurate as possible; (ii) intermediate assessment results can be used, for example, to support risk assessments at other tiers; and (iii) the results are meaningful and useful inputs to the risk response step in the risk management process. The manner and form in which risks are communicated are an expression of organizational culture as well as legal, regulatory, and contractual constraints. To be effective, communication of information security risks and other risk-related information produced during the risk assessment is consistent with other forms of risk communication within organizations. To maximize the benefit of risk assessments, organizations should establish policies, procedures, and implementing mechanisms to ensure that the information produced during such assessments is effectively communicated and shared across all three risk management tiers.[42] To reinforce the importance of risk communication and information sharing within organizations, the input tables in Appendices D, E, F, G, H, and I (i.e., threat sources, threat events, vulnerabilities, predisposing conditions, likelihood, impact, and risk) and the recommended elements of a risk assessment report (Appendix K) provide recommendations for risk communication/sharing among the tiers.

TARGETED RISK ASSESSMENTS

Organizations can use *targeted* risk assessments, in which the scope is narrowly defined, to produce answers to specific questions (e.g., what is the risk associated with relying on a given technology, how should prior assessments of risk be revised based on incidents that have occurred, what new risks can be identified based on knowledge about a newly discovered threat or vulnerability) or to inform specific decisions (e.g., which risks should be managed at Tier 1 rather than Tier 2 or 3). Organizations may consider assessing risk at Tier 1 and Tier 2 arising from a set of common threats and vulnerabilities applicable to a wide range of organizational information systems. Assessing risk at Tiers 1 and 2 allows organizations to reduce the number of threats and vulnerabilities considered at the individual information system level and develop common risk responses for such organization-wide risks. This approach can support the common control selection process for organizations and increase the efficiency and cost-effectiveness of risk assessments across the organization.

With respect to all three tiers in the risk management hierarchy, there are *no specific requirements* with regard to: (i) the formality, rigor, or level of detail that characterizes any particular risk assessment; (ii) the methodologies, tools, and techniques used to conduct such risk assessments; or (iii) the format and content of assessment results and any associated reporting mechanisms. Organizations have *maximum flexibility* on how risk assessments are conducted, where such assessments are applied, and how the results will be used. Organizations are encouraged to use the guidance in a manner that most effectively and cost-effectively provides the information necessary to senior leaders/executives to facilitate informed risk management decisions.

---

[42] NIST Special Publications 800-117 and 800-126 provide guidance on the Security Content Automation Protocol (SCAP) program. The SCAP program provides a standard, consistent way to communicate threat and vulnerability information.

CHAPTER THREE

THE PROCESS

CONDUCTING RISK ASSESSMENTS WITHIN ORGANIZATIONS

This chapter describes the process of assessing information security risk including: (i) a high-level overview of the risk assessment process; (ii) the activities necessary to prepare for risk assessments; (iii) the activities necessary to conduct effective risk assessments; (iv) the activities necessary to communicate the assessment results and share risk-related information; and (v) the activities necessary to maintain the results of risk assessments on an ongoing basis. The risk assessment process[43] is composed of four steps: (i) *prepare* for the assessment; (ii) *conduct* the assessment; (iii) *communicate* assessment results; and (iv) *maintain* the assessment.[44] Each step is divided into a set of tasks. For each task, supplemental guidance provides additional information for organizations conducting risk assessments. Risk tables and exemplary assessment scales are listed in appropriate tasks and cross-referenced to additional, more detailed information in the supporting appendices. Figure 5 illustrates the basic steps in the risk assessment process and highlights the specific tasks for conducting the assessment.

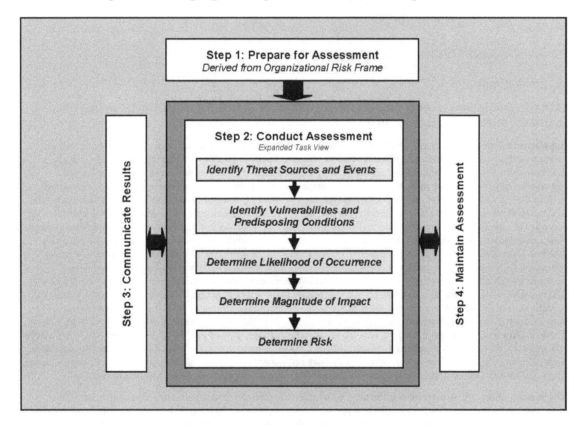

FIGURE 5: RISK ASSESSMENT PROCESS

---

[43] The intent of the process description in Chapter Three is to provide a common expression of the essential elements of an effective risk assessment. It is not intended to limit organizational flexibility in conducting those assessments. Other procedures can be implemented if organizations choose to do so, consistent with the intent of the process description.

[44] The four-step risk assessment process described in this publication is consistent with the general risk assessment process described in NIST Special Publication 800-39. The additional steps and tasks result from the need to provide more detailed guidance to effectively carry out the specific activities associated with risk assessments.

3.1 PREPARING FOR THE RISK ASSESSMENT

The first step in the risk assessment process is to *prepare* for the assessment. The objective of this step is to establish a context for the risk assessment. This context is established and informed by the results from the risk framing step of the risk management process. Risk framing identifies, for example, organizational information regarding policies and requirements for conducting risk assessments, specific assessment methodologies to be employed, procedures for selecting risk factors to be considered, scope of the assessments, rigor of analyses, degree of formality, and requirements that facilitate consistent and repeatable risk determinations across the organization. Organizations use the risk management strategy to the extent practicable to obtain information to prepare for the risk assessment. Preparing for a risk assessment includes the following tasks:

- Identify the purpose of the assessment;

- Identify the scope of the assessment;

- Identify the assumptions and constraints associated with the assessment;

- Identify the sources of information to be used as inputs to the assessment; and

- Identify the risk model and analytic approaches (i.e., assessment and analysis approaches) to be employed during the assessment.

STEP 1: PREPARE FOR THE ASSESSMENT

IDENTIFY PURPOSE

TASK 1-1: Identify the purpose of the risk assessment in terms of the information that the assessment is intended to produce and the decisions the assessment is intended to support.

Supplemental Guidance: The purpose of the risk assessment is explicitly stated in sufficient detail to ensure that the assessment produces the appropriate information and supports the intended decisions. Organizations can provide guidance on how to capture and present information produced during the risk assessment (e.g., using a defined organizational template). Appendix K provides an exemplary template for a risk assessment report or the preferred vehicle for risk communication. At Tier 3, risk assessments support: (i) authorization-related decisions throughout the system development life cycle; (ii) reciprocity, particularly for reuse of assessment information; (iii) risk management activities at Tier 2; and (iv) programmatic risk management activities throughout the system development life cycle. At Tier 2, risk assessments enable organizations to: (i) understand dependencies and ways in which risks are accepted, rejected, shared, transferred, or mitigated among information systems that support organizational mission/business processes; (ii) support architectural and operational decisions for organizational risk responses (e.g., reducing dependencies, limiting connectivity, enhancing or focusing monitoring, and enhancing information/system resiliency); (iii) identify trends, so that proactive risk response strategies and courses of action for mission/business processes can be defined; and (iv) support reciprocity, particularly to enable information sharing. At Tier 1, risk assessments: (i) support the risk executive (function); and (ii) serve as a key input to the risk management strategy. In addition to these common purposes, risk assessments may have a very specific purpose, to answer a specific question (e.g., What are the risk implications of a newly discovered vulnerability or class of vulnerabilities, allowing new connectivity, outsourcing a specific function, or adopting a new technology?). Risk assessment results from all tiers can be used by organizations to inform the acquisition process by helping to ensure information security requirements are clearly specified.

The purpose of the risk assessment is influenced by whether the assessment is: (i) an initial assessment; or (ii) a subsequent assessment initiated from the risk response or monitoring steps in the risk management process. For initial assessments, the purpose can include, for example: (i) establishing a baseline assessment of risk; or (ii) identifying threats and vulnerabilities, impacts to organizational operations and assets, individuals, other organizations, and the Nation, and other risk factors to be tracked over time as part of risk monitoring. For a reassessment initiated from the risk response step, the purpose can include, for example, providing a comparative analysis of alternative risk responses or answering a specific question (see discussion of *targeted risk assessments* above). Alternatively, for a reassessment initiated from the risk monitoring step, the purpose can include, for example, updating the risk assessment based on: (i) ongoing determinations of the effectiveness of security controls in organizational information systems or environments of operation; (ii) changes to information systems or environments of operation (e.g., changes to hardware, firmware, software; changes to system-specific, hybrid, or common controls; changes to mission/business processes, common infrastructure and support services, threats, vulnerabilities, or facilities); and (iii) results from compliance verification activities. Reassessments can also be initiated by organizations due to incidents that have occurred (e.g., cyber attacks compromising organizational information or information systems).

IDENTIFY SCOPE

TASK 1-2: Identify the scope of the risk assessment in terms of organizational applicability, time frame supported, and architectural/technology considerations.

Supplemental Guidance: The scope of the risk assessment determines what will be considered in the assessment. Risk assessment scope affects the range of information available to make risk-based decisions and is determined by the organizational official requesting the assessment and the risk management strategy. Establishing the scope of the risk assessment helps organizations to determine: (i) what tiers are addressed in the assessment; (ii) what parts of organizations are affected by the assessment and how they are affected; (iii) what decisions the assessment results support; (iv) how long assessment results are relevant; and (v) what influences the need to update the assessment. Establishing the scope of the risk assessment helps to determine the form and content of the risk assessment report, as well as the information to be shared as a result of conducting the assessment. At Tier 3, the scope of a risk assessment can depend on the authorization boundary for the information system. Appendix K provides an example of the type of information that may be included in a risk assessment report or the preferred vehicle for risk communication.

Organizational Applicability

Organizational applicability describes which parts of the organization or suborganizations are affected by the risk assessment and the risk-based decisions resulting from the assessment (including the parts of the organization or suborganizations responsible for implementing the activities and tasks related to the decisions). For example, the risk assessment can inform decisions regarding information systems supporting a particular organizational mission/business function or mission/business process. This can include decisions regarding the selection, tailoring, or supplementation of security controls for specific information systems or the selection of common controls. Alternatively, the risk assessment can inform decisions regarding a set of closely related missions/business functions or mission/business processes. The scope of the risk assessment can include not only the missions/business functions, mission/business processes, common infrastructure, or shared services on which the organization currently depends, but also those which the organization might use under specific operational conditions.

Effectiveness Time Frame

Organizations determine how long the results of particular risk assessments can be used to legitimately inform risk-based decisions. The time frame is usually related to the purpose of the assessment. For example, a risk assessment to inform Tier 1 policy-related decisions needs to be relevant for an extended period of time since the governance process for policy changes can be time-consuming in many organizations. A risk assessment conducted to inform a Tier 3 decision on the use of a compensating security control for an information system may be relevant only until the next release of the information technology product providing the required security capability. Organizations determine the useful life of risk assessment results and under what conditions the current assessment results become ineffective or irrelevant. Risk monitoring can be used to help determine the effectiveness of time frames for risk assessments. In addition to risk assessment results, organizations also consider the currency/timeliness (i.e., latency or age) of all types of information/data used in assessing risk. This is of particular concern in information reuse and evaluating the validity of assessment results.

Architectural/Technology Considerations

Organizations use architectural and technology considerations to clarify the scope of the risk assessment. For example, at Tier 3, the scope of the risk assessment can be an organizational information system in its environment of operations. This entails placing the information system in its architectural context, so that vulnerabilities in inherited controls can be taken into consideration. Alternately, the scope of the assessment can be limited solely to the information system, without consideration of inherited vulnerabilities. At Tier 2, the scope of the risk assessment can be defined in terms of the mission/business segment architecture (e.g., including all systems, services, and infrastructures that support a specific mission/function). For a targeted risk assessment at any tier, the specific question to be answered can restrict the scope to a specific technology.

IDENTIFY ASSUMPTIONS AND CONSTRAINTS

TASK 1-3: Identify the specific assumptions and constraints under which the risk assessment is conducted.

Supplemental Guidance: As part of the risk framing step in the risk management process, organizations make explicit the specific assumptions, constraints, risk tolerance, and priorities/trade-offs used within organizations to make investment and operational decisions. This information guides and informs organizational risk assessments. When an organizational risk management strategy cannot be cited, risk assessments identify and document assumptions and constraints. Assumptions and constraints identified by organizations during the risk framing step and included as part of the organizational risk management strategy need not be repeated in each individual risk assessment. By making assumptions and constraints explicit, there is greater clarity in the risk model selected for the risk assessment, increased reproducibility/repeatability of assessment results, and an increased opportunity for reciprocity among organizations. Organizations identify assumptions in key areas relevant to the risk assessment including, for example: (i) threat sources; (ii) threat events; (iii) vulnerabilities and predisposing conditions; (iv) potential impacts; (v) assessment and analysis approaches; and (vi) which missions/business functions are primary. Organizations also identify constraints in key areas relevant to the risk assessment including, for example: (i) resources available for the assessment; (ii) skills and expertise required for the assessment; and (iii) operational considerations related to mission/business activities. For example, organizational assumptions about how threats and impacts should be assessed can range from using worst-case projections to using best-case projections or anything in between those endpoints. Finally, organizations consider the uncertainty with regard to assumptions made or other information used in the risk assessment. Uncertainty in assumptions can affect organizational risk tolerance. For example, assumptions based on a lack of specific or credible information may reduce an organization's risk tolerance because of the uncertainty influencing the assumptions. The following sections provide some representative examples of areas where assumptions/constraints for risk assessments may be identified.

Threat Sources

Organizations determine which types of threat sources are to be considered during risk assessments. Organizations make explicit the process used to identify threats and any assumptions related to the threat identification process. If such information is identified during the risk framing step and included as part of the organizational risk management strategy, the information need not be repeated in each individual risk assessment. Risk assessments can address all types of threat sources, a single broad threat source (e.g., adversarial), or a specific threat source (e.g., trusted insider). Table D-2 provides a sample taxonomy of threat sources that can be considered by organizations in identifying assumptions for risk assessments. Organizational assumptions about threat sources to consider inform Task 2-1.

Threat Events

Organizations determine which type of threat events are to be considered during risk assessments and the level of detail needed to describe such events. Descriptions of threat events can be expressed in highly general terms (e.g., phishing, distributed denial-of-service), in more descriptive terms using tactics, techniques, and procedures, or in highly specific terms (e.g., the names of specific information systems, technologies, organizations, roles, or locations). In addition, organizations consider: (i) what representative set of threat events can serve as a starting point for the identification of the specific threat events in the risk assessment; and (ii) what degree of confirmation is needed for threat events to be considered relevant for purposes of the risk assessment. For example, organizations may consider only those threat events that have been observed (either internally or by organizations that are peers/partners) or all possible threat events. Table E-2 and Table E-3 provide representative examples of adversarial and non-adversarial threat events at a level of detail that can be used for risk assessments at all tiers. Greater detail can be found in multiple sources (e.g., Common Attack Pattern Enumeration and Classification [CAPEC]). Organizational assumptions about threat events to consider and level of detail, inform Task 2-2.

Vulnerabilities and Predisposing Conditions

Organizations determine the types of vulnerabilities that are to be considered during risk assessments and the level of detail provided in the vulnerability descriptions. Organizations make explicit the process used to identify vulnerabilities and any assumptions related to the vulnerability identification process. If such information is identified during the risk framing step and included as part of the organizational risk management strategy, the information need not be repeated in each individual risk assessment. Vulnerabilities can be associated with organizational information systems (e.g., hardware, software, firmware, internal controls, and security procedures) or the environments in which those systems operate (e.g., organizational governance, external relationships, mission/business processes, enterprise architectures, information security architectures). Organizations also determine the types of predisposing conditions that are to be considered during risk assessments including, for example, architectures and technologies employed, environments of operation, and personnel. Table F-4 provides representative examples of such predisposing conditions. Organizational assumptions about vulnerabilities and predisposing conditions to consider and level of detail, inform Task 2-3.

Likelihood

Organizations make explicit the process used to conduct likelihood determinations and any assumptions related to the likelihood determination process. If such information is identified during the risk framing step and included as part of the organizational risk management strategy, the information need not be repeated in each individual risk assessment. Organizational assumptions about how to determine likelihood inform Task 2-4.

Impacts

Organizations determine potential adverse impacts in terms of organizational operations (i.e., missions, functions, image, and reputation), organizational assets, individuals, other organizations, and the Nation. Organizations make explicit the process used to conduct impact determinations and any assumptions related to the impact determination process. If such information is identified during the risk framing step and included as part of the organizational risk management strategy, the information need not be repeated in each individual risk assessment. Organizations address impacts at a level of detail that includes, for example, specific mission/business processes or information resources (e.g., information, personnel, equipment, funds, and information technology). Organizations may include information from Business Impact Analyses with regard to providing impact information for risk assessments. Table H-2 provides representative examples of types of impacts (i.e., harm) that can be considered by organizations. Organizational assumptions about how to determine impacts and at what level of detail, inform Task 2-5.

Risk Tolerance and Uncertainty

Organizations determine the levels and types of risk that are acceptable. Risk tolerance is determined as part of the organizational risk management strategy to ensure consistency across the organization. Organizations also provide guidance on how to identify reasons for uncertainty when risk factors are assessed, since uncertainty in one or more factors will propagate to the resulting evaluation of level of risk, and how to compensate for incomplete, imperfect, or assumption-dependent estimates. Consideration of uncertainty is especially important when organizations consider advanced persistent threats (APT) since assessments of the likelihood of threat event occurrence can have a great degree of uncertainty. To compensate, organizations can take a variety of approaches to determine likelihood, ranging from assuming the worst-case likelihood (certain to happen sometime in the foreseeable future) to assuming that if an event has not been observed, it is unlikely to happen. Organizations also determine what levels of risk (combination of likelihood and impact) indicate that no further analysis of any risk factors is needed.

Analytic Approach

Risk assessments include both assessment approaches (i.e., quantitative, qualitative, semi-quantitative) and analysis approaches (i.e., threat-oriented, asset/impact-oriented, vulnerability-oriented). Together, the assessment and analysis approaches form the *analytic approach* for the risk assessment. Organizations determine the level of detail and in what form, threats are analyzed including the level of granularity to describe threat events or threat scenarios. Different analysis approaches can lead to different levels of detail in characterizing adverse events for which likelihoods are determined. For example, an adverse event could be characterized in several ways (with increasing levels of detail): (i) a threat event (for which the likelihood is determined by taking the maximum overall threat sources); (ii) a pairing of a threat event and a threat source; or (iii) a detailed threat scenario/attack tree. In general, organizations can be expected to require more detail for highly critical missions/business functions, common infrastructures, or shared services on which multiple missions or business functions depend (as common points of failure), and information systems with high criticality or sensitivity. Mission/business owners may amplify this guidance for risk *hot spots* (information systems, services, or critical infrastructure components of particular concern) in mission/business segments.

IDENTIFY INFORMATION SOURCES

TASK 1-4: Identify the sources of descriptive, threat, vulnerability, and impact information to be used in the risk assessment.

Supplemental Guidance: Descriptive information enables organizations to be able to determine the relevance of threat and vulnerability information. At Tier 1, descriptive information can include, for example, the type of risk management and information security governance structures in place within organizations and how the organization identifies and prioritizes critical missions/business functions. At Tier 2, descriptive information can include, for example, information about: (i) organizational mission/business processes, functional management processes, and information flows; (ii) enterprise architecture, information security architecture, and the technical/process flow architectures of the systems, common infrastructures, and shared services that fall within the scope of the risk assessment; and (iii) the external environments in which organizations operate including, for example, the relationships and dependencies with external providers. Such information is typically found in architectural documentation (particularly documentation of high-level operational views), business continuity plans, and risk assessment reports for organizational information systems, common infrastructures, and shared services that fall within the scope of the risk assessment. At Tier 3, descriptive information can include, for example, information about: (i) the design of and technologies used in organizational information systems; (ii) the environment in which the systems operate; (iii) connectivity to and dependency on other information systems; and (iv) dependencies on common infrastructures or shared services. Such information is found in system documentation, contingency plans, and risk assessment reports for other information systems, infrastructures, and services.

Sources of information as described in Tables D-1, E-1, F-1, H-1, and I-1 can be either internal or external to organizations. Internal sources of information that can provide insights into both threats and vulnerabilities can include, for example, risk assessment reports, incident reports, security logs, trouble tickets, and monitoring results. Note that internally, information from risk assessment reports at one tier can serve as input to risk assessments at other tiers. Mission/business owners are encouraged to identify not only common infrastructure and/or support services they depend on, but also those they might use under specific operational circumstances. External sources of threat information can include cross-community organizations (e.g., US Computer Emergency Readiness Team [US-CERT], sector partners (e.g., Defense Industrial Base [DIB] using the DoD-Defense Industrial Base Collaborative Information

Sharing Environment [DCISE], Information Sharing and Analysis Centers [ISACs] for critical infrastructure sectors), research and nongovernmental organizations (e.g. Carnegie Mellon University, Software Engineering Institute-CERT), and security service providers). Organizations using external sources, consider the timeliness, specificity, and relevance of threat information. Similar to sources of threat information, sources of vulnerability information can also be either internal or external to organizations (see Table F-1). Internal sources can include, for example, vulnerability assessment reports. External sources of vulnerability information are similar to the sources identified above for threat information. As described in Table F-1, information about predisposing conditions can be found in a variety of sources including, for example, descriptions of information systems, environments of operation, shared services, common infrastructures, and enterprise architecture. As described in Table H-1, sources of impact information can include, for example, mission/business impact analyses, information system component inventories, and security categorizations. Security categorization constitutes a determination of the potential impacts should certain events occur which jeopardize the information and information systems needed by the organization to accomplish its assigned missions, protect its assets, fulfill its legal responsibilities, maintain its day-to-day functions, and protect individuals. Security categories are to be used in conjunction with vulnerability and threat information in assessing the risk to organizational operations and assets, individuals, other organizations, and the Nation. Security categories constitute an initial summary of impact in terms of failures to meet the security objectives of confidentiality, integrity, and availability, and are informed by the types of harm presented in Table H-2.

IDENTIFY RISK MODEL AND ANALYTIC APPROACH

TASK 1-5: Identify the risk model and analytic approach to be used in the risk assessment.

Supplemental Guidance: Organizations define one or more risk models for use in conducting risk assessments (see Section 2.3.1) and identify which model is to be used for the risk assessment. To facilitate reciprocity of assessment results, organization-specific risk models include, or can be translated into, the risk factors (i.e., threat, vulnerability, impact, likelihood, and predisposing condition) defined in the appendices. Organizations also identify the specific analytic approach to be used for the risk assessment including the assessment approach (i.e., quantitative, qualitative, semi-quantitative) and the analysis approach (i.e., threat-oriented, asset/impact-oriented, vulnerability-oriented). For each assessable risk factor, the appendices include three assessment scales (one qualitative and two semi-quantitative scales) with correspondingly different representations. Organizations typically define (or select and tailor from the appendices) the assessment scales to be used in their risk assessments, annotating with organizationally-meaningful examples for specific values and defining break points between bins for semi-quantitative approaches. In addition, mission/business owners can provide further annotations with mission/business-specific examples. Organizations can identify different assessment scales to be used in different circumstances. For example, for low-impact information systems, organizations could use qualitative values, while for moderate- and high-impact systems, the most granular semi-quantitative values (0-100) could be used. As discussed in Special Publication 800-39, Task 1-1, Risk Assumptions, organizations vary in the relative weights applied to risk factors. Therefore, this guideline does not specify algorithms for combining semi-quantitative values. Organization-specific risk models include algorithms (e.g., formulas, tables, rules) for combining risk factors. If an organization-specific risk model is not provided in the risk management strategy as part of the risk framing step, then part of this task is to specify the algorithms for combining values. Algorithms for combining risk factors reflect organizational risk tolerance (see the supplemental guidance to Task 2-4 for examples). Organization-specific risk models are refined as part of preparation for a risk assessment by: (i) identifying the risk model and the rationale for using it (when multiple organization-specific risk models are provided); (ii) providing additional examples for values of risk factors; and (iii) identifying any assessment-specific algorithms (e.g., algorithms specific to the use of an attack graph analysis technique). In the absence of pre-existing organization-specific risk models or analytic approaches defined in the organizational risk management strategy, the risk model and analytic approaches to be used in the risk assessment are defined and documented in this task.

Summary of Key Activities – Preparing for Risk Assessments

- Identify the *purpose* of the risk assessment.

- Identify the *scope* of the risk assessment.

- Identify the *assumptions* and *constraints* under which the risk assessment is conducted.

- Identify *sources* of threat, vulnerability, and impact information to be used in the risk assessment (see Tables D-1, E-1, F-1, H-1, and I-1 as tailored by the organization).

- Define or refine the *risk model*, *assessment approach*, and *analysis approach* to be used in the risk assessment.

3.2 CONDUCTING THE RISK ASSESSMENT

The second step in the risk assessment process is to *conduct* the assessment. The objective of this step is to produce a list of information security risks that can be prioritized by risk level and used to inform risk response decisions. To accomplish this objective, organizations analyze threats and vulnerabilities, impacts and likelihood, and the uncertainty associated with the risk assessment process. This step also includes the gathering of essential information as a part of each task and is conducted in accordance with the assessment context established in the Prepare step of the risk assessment process. The expectation for risk assessments is to adequately cover the entire threat space in accordance with the specific definitions, guidance, and direction established during the Prepare step. However, in practice, adequate coverage within available resources may dictate generalizing threat sources, threat events, and vulnerabilities to ensure full coverage and assessing specific, detailed sources, events, and vulnerabilities only as necessary to accomplish risk assessment objectives. Conducting risk assessments includes the following specific tasks:

- Identify threat sources that are relevant to organizations;

- Identify threat events that could be produced by those sources;

- Identify vulnerabilities within organizations that could be exploited by threat sources through specific threat events and the predisposing conditions that could affect successful exploitation;

- Determine the likelihood that the identified threat sources would initiate specific threat events and the likelihood that the threat events would be successful;

- Determine the adverse impacts to organizational operations and assets, individuals, other organizations, and the Nation resulting from the exploitation of vulnerabilities by threat sources (through specific threat events); and

- Determine information security risks as a combination of likelihood of threat exploitation of vulnerabilities and the impact of such exploitation, including any uncertainties associated with the risk determinations.

The specific tasks are presented in a sequential manner for clarity. However, in practice, some iteration among the tasks is both necessary and expected.[45] Depending on the purpose of the risk assessment, organizations may find reordering the tasks advantageous.[46] Whatever adjustments organizations make to the tasks described below, risk assessments should meet the stated purpose, scope, assumptions, and constraints established by the organizations initiating the assessments. To assist organizations in executing the individual tasks in the risk assessment process, a set of templates is provided in Appendices D through I. These appendices provide useful information for organizations in assessing risk and can also be used to record assessment results produced during essential calculations and analyses. The templates are exemplary and can be tailored by organizations in accordance with specific organizational mission/business requirements. The use of the templates is not required in order to conduct risk assessments.

---

[45] For example, as vulnerabilities are identified, additional threat events might be identified by asking how the newly identified vulnerabilities could be exploited. If organizations identify vulnerabilities first and then define threat events, there may be some events that do not map cleanly to vulnerabilities but do map to predisposing conditions.

[46] For example, the risk assessment could start with an identification of mission/business impacts at Tiers 1 and 2 using common techniques such as Mission Impact Analyses, Business Impact Analyses, Mission/Business Thread Analyses, or Business Continuity Analyses. The results of such analyses could enable risk assessors to focus attention on, and perform more detailed analysis of, potential threats to critical information systems, databases, communications links, or other assets.

STEP 2: CONDUCT THE ASSESSMENT

IDENTIFY THREAT SOURCES

TASK 2-1: Identify and characterize threat sources of concern, including capability, intent, and targeting characteristics for adversarial threats and range of effects for non-adversarial threats.

Supplemental Guidance: Organizations identify threat sources of concern and determine the characteristics associated with those threat sources. For adversarial threat sources, assess the capabilities, intentions, and targeting associated with the threat sources. For non-adversarial threat sources, assess the potential range of effects from the threat sources. The risk management strategy and the results of the Prepare step provide organizational direction and guidance for conducting threat source identification and characterization including, for example: (i) sources for obtaining threat information; (ii) threat sources to consider (by type/name); (iii) threat taxonomy to be used; and (iv) the process for identifying which threat sources are of concern for the risk assessment. As identified in Task 1-3, organizations make explicit any assumptions concerning threat sources including decisions regarding the identification of threat sources when specific and credible threat information is unavailable. Organizations can also view adversarial threat sources from a broad-based perspective, considering the time such threat sources may have to exploit identified organizational vulnerabilities, the scale of the attack, and the potential use of multiple attack vectors. The identification and characterization of Advanced Persistent Threats (APTs) can involve considerable uncertainty. Organizations annotate such threat sources with appropriate rationale and references (and providing classifications as necessary).

Appendix D provides a set of exemplary tables for use in identifying threat sources:

- Table D-1 provides a set of exemplary inputs to the threat source identification task;
- Table D-2 provides an exemplary taxonomy that can be used to identify and characterize threat sources;
- Tables D-3, D-4, and D-5 provide exemplary assessment scales to assess the risk factors (i.e., characteristics) of adversarial threat sources with regard to capability, intent, and targeting;
- Table D-6 provides an exemplary assessment scale for assessing the ranges of effects from threat events initiated by non-adversarial threat sources; and
- Tables D-7 and D-8 provide templates for summarizing and documenting the results of threat source identification and characterization.

If a particular type of threat source is outside the scope of the risk assessment or not relevant to the organization, the information in Tables D-7 and D-8 can be truncated accordingly. The information produced in Task 2-1 provides threat source inputs to the risk tables in Appendix I.

Summary of Key Activities – Task 2-1

- Identify threat source inputs (see **Table D-1**, as tailored by the organization).

- Identify threat sources (see **Table D-2**, as tailored by the organization).

- Determine if threat sources are relevant to the organization and in scope (see **Table D-1**, as tailored by the organization).

- Create or update the assessment of threat sources (see **Table D-7** for adversarial threat sources and **Table D-8** for non-adversarial threat sources, as tailored by the organization).

  - For relevant adversarial threat sources:

    - Assess adversary capability (see **Table D-3**, as tailored by the organization).

    - Assess adversary intent (see **Table D-4**, as tailored by the organization).

    - Assess adversary targeting (see **Table D-5**, as tailored by the organization).

  - For relevant non-adversarial threat sources:

    - Assess the range of effects from threat sources (see **Table D-6**, as tailored by the organization).

IDENTIFY THREAT EVENTS

TASK 2-2: Identify potential threat events, relevance of the events, and the threat sources that could initiate the events.

Supplemental Guidance: Threat events are characterized by the threat sources that could initiate the events, and for adversarial events, the TTPs used to carry out attacks. Organizations define these threat events with sufficient detail to accomplish the purpose of the risk assessment. At Tier 1, threat events that could affect the organizational level are of particular interest. At Tier 2, threat events that cross or span information system boundaries, exploit functional dependencies or connectivity among systems, or affect mission/business owners, are of particular interest. At Tier 3, threat events that can be described in terms of specific information systems, technologies, or environments of operation are of particular interest. Multiple threat sources can initiate a single threat event. Conversely, a single threat source can potentially initiate any of multiple threat events. Therefore, there can be a many-to-many relationship among threat events and threat sources that can potentially increase the complexity of the risk assessment. To enable effective use and communication of risk assessment results, organizations tailor the general descriptions of threat events in Tables E-2 and E-3 to identify how each event could potentially harm organizational operations (including mission, functions, image, or reputation) and assets, individuals, other organizations, or the Nation. For each threat event identified, organizations determine the relevance of the event. Table E-4 provides a range of values for relevance of threat events. The values selected by organizations have a direct linkage to organizational risk tolerance. The more risk averse, the greater the range of values considered. Organizations accepting greater risk or having a greater risk tolerance are more likely to require substantive evidence before giving serious consideration to threat events. If a threat event is deemed to be irrelevant, no further consideration is given. For relevant threat events, organizations identify all potential threat sources that could initiate the events. For use in Task 2-4, organizations can identify each pairing of threat source and threat event separately since the likelihood of threat initiation and success could be different for each pairing. Alternatively, organizations can identify the set of all possible threat sources that could potentially initiate a threat event.

Appendix E provides a set of exemplary tables for use in identifying threat events:

- Table E-1 provides a set of exemplary inputs to the threat event identification task;

- Table E-2 provides representative examples of adversarial threat events expressed as TTPs;

- Table E-3 provides representative examples of non-adversarial threat events;

- Table E-4 provides exemplary values for the relevance of threat events to organizations; and

- Table E-5 provides a template for summarizing and documenting the results of threat event identification.

The information produced in Task 2-2 provides threat event inputs to the risk tables in Appendix I.

Summary of Key Activities – Task 2-2

- Identify threat event inputs (see **Table E-1**, as tailored by the organization).

- Identify threat events (see **Table E-2** for adversarial threat events and **Table E-3** for non-adversarial threat events, as tailored by the organization); create or update **Table E-5**.

- Identify threat sources that could initiate the threat events (see **Table D-7** and **Table D-8**, as tailored by the organization); update **Table E-5**.

- Assess the relevance of threat events to the organization (see **Table E-4**, as tailored by the organization); update **Table E-5**.

- Update Columns 1-6 in **Table I-5** for adversarial risk (see **Table E-5** and **Table D-7**); or update Columns 1-4 in **Table I-7** for non-adversarial risk (see **Table E-5** and **Table D-8**).

IDENTIFY VULNERABILITIES AND PREDISPOSING CONDITIONS

TASK 2-3: Identify vulnerabilities and predisposing conditions that affect the likelihood that threat events of concern result in adverse impacts.

Supplemental Guidance: The primary purpose of vulnerability assessments is to understand the nature and degree to which organizations, mission/business processes, and information systems are vulnerable to threat sources identified in Task 2-1 and the threat events identified in Task 2-2 that can be initiated by those threat sources. Vulnerabilities at Tier 1 can be pervasive across organizations and can have wide-ranging adverse impacts if exploited by threat events. For example, organizational failure to consider supply chain activities can result in organizations acquiring subverted components that adversaries could exploit to disrupt organizational missions/business functions or to obtain sensitive organizational information. Vulnerabilities at Tier 2 can be described in terms of organizational mission/business processes, enterprise architecture, the use of multiple information systems, or common infrastructures/shared services. At Tier 2, vulnerabilities typically cross or span information system boundaries. Vulnerabilities at Tier 3 can be described in terms of the information technologies employed within organizational information systems, the environments in which those systems operate, and/or the lack of or weaknesses in system-specific security controls. There is potentially a many-to-many relationship between threat events and vulnerabilities. Multiple threat events can exploit a single vulnerability, and conversely, multiple vulnerabilities can be exploited by a single threat event. The severity of a vulnerability is an assessment of the relative importance of mitigating such a vulnerability. Initially, the extent to which mitigation is unplanned can serve as a surrogate for vulnerability severity. Once the risks associated with a particular vulnerability have been assessed, the impact severity and exposure of the vulnerability given the security controls implemented and other vulnerabilities can be taken into consideration in assessing vulnerability severity. Assessments of vulnerability severity support risk response. Vulnerabilities can be identified at varying degrees of granularity and specificity. The level of detail provided in any particular vulnerability assessment is consistent with the purpose of the risk assessment and the type of inputs needed to support follow-on likelihood and impact determinations.

Due to the ever-increasing size and complexity of organizations, mission/business processes, and the information systems supporting those processes, the number of vulnerabilities tends to be large and can increase the overall complexity of the analysis. Therefore, organizations have the option of using the vulnerability identification task to understand the general nature of the vulnerabilities (including scope, number, and type) relevant to the assessment (see Task 1-3) and performing a cataloging of specific vulnerabilities as necessary to do so. Organizations determine which vulnerabilities are relevant to which threat events in order to reduce the space of potential risks to be assessed. In addition to identifying vulnerabilities, organizations also identify any predisposing conditions which may affect susceptibility to certain vulnerabilities. Predisposing conditions that exist within organizations (including mission/business processes, information systems, and environments of operation) can contribute to (i.e., increase or decrease) the likelihood that one or more threat events, once initiated by threat sources, result in adverse impacts to organizational operations, organizational assets, individuals, other organizations, or the Nation. Organizations determine which predisposing conditions are relevant to which threat events in order to reduce the space of potential risks to be assessed. Organizations assess the pervasiveness of predisposing conditions to support determination of the tier(s) at which risk response could be most effective.

Appendix F provides a set of exemplary tables for use in identifying vulnerabilities and predisposing conditions:

- Table F-1 provides a set of exemplary inputs to the vulnerability and predisposing condition identification task;

- Table F-2 provides an exemplary assessment scale for assessing the severity of identified vulnerabilities;

- Table F-3 provides a template for summarizing/documenting the results of vulnerability identification;

- Table F-4 provides an exemplary taxonomy that can be used to identify and characterize predisposing conditions;

- Table F-5 provides an exemplary assessment scale for assessing the pervasiveness of predisposing conditions; and

- Table F-6 provides a template for summarizing/documenting the results of identifying predisposing conditions.

The information produced in Task 2-3 provides vulnerability and predisposing condition inputs to the risk tables in Appendix I.

Summary of Key Activities – Task 2-3

- Identify vulnerability and predisposing condition inputs (see **Table F-1**, as tailored by the organization).

- Identify vulnerabilities using organization-defined information sources; create or update **Table F-3**.

- Assess the severity of identified vulnerabilities (see **Table F-2**, as tailored by the organization); update **Table F-3**.

- Identify predisposing conditions (see **Table F-4**, as tailored by the organization); create or update **Table F-6**.

- Assess the pervasiveness of predisposing conditions (see **Table F-5**, as tailored by the organization); update **Table F-6**.

- Update Column 8 in **Table I-5** for adversarial risk; or update Column 6 in **Table I-7** for non-adversarial risk (see **Table F-3** and **Table F-6**).

- Update Column 9 in **Table I-5** for adversarial risk; or update Column 7 in **Table I-7** for non-adversarial risk (see **Table F-2** and **Table F-5**).

DETERMINE LIKELIHOOD

TASK 2-4: Determine the likelihood that threat events of concern result in adverse impacts, considering: (i) the characteristics of the threat sources that could initiate the events; (ii) the vulnerabilities/predisposing conditions identified; and (iii) the organizational susceptibility reflecting the safeguards/countermeasures planned or implemented to impede such events.

Supplemental Guidance: Organizations employ a three-step process to determine the overall likelihood of threat events. First, organizations assess the likelihood that threat events will be initiated (for adversarial threat events) or will occur (for non-adversarial threat events). Second, organizations assess the likelihood that threat events once initiated or occurring, will result in adverse impacts to organizational operations and assets, individuals, other organizations, or the Nation. Finally, organizations assess the overall likelihood as a combination of likelihood of initiation/occurrence and likelihood of resulting in adverse impact.

Organizations assess the likelihood of threat event initiation by taking into consideration the characteristics of the threat sources of concern including capability, intent, and targeting (see Task 2-1 and Appendix D). If threat events require more capability than adversaries possess (and adversaries are cognizant of this fact), then the adversaries are not expected to initiate the events. If adversaries do not expect to achieve intended objectives by executing threat events, then the adversaries are not expected to initiate the events. And finally, if adversaries are not actively targeting specific organizations or their missions/business functions, adversaries are not expected to initiate threat events. Organizations use the assessment scale in Table G-2 and provide a rationale for the assessment allowing explicit consideration of deterrence and threat shifting. Organizations can assess the likelihood of threat event occurrence (non-adversarial) using Table G-3 and provide a similar rationale for the assessment.

Organizations assess the likelihood that threat events result in adverse impacts by taking into consideration the set of identified vulnerabilities and predisposing conditions (see Task 2-3 and Appendix F). For threat events initiated by adversaries, organizations consider characteristics of associated threat sources. For non-adversarial threat events, organizations take into account the anticipated severity and duration of the event (as included in the description of the event). Organizations use the assessment scale in Table G-4 and provide a rationale for the assessment allowing explicit consideration as stated above. Threat events for which no vulnerabilities or predisposing conditions are identified, have a very low likelihood of resulting in adverse impacts. Such threat events can be highlighted and moved to the end of the table (or to a separate table), so that they can be tracked for consideration in follow-on risk assessments. However, no further consideration during the current assessment is warranted.

The *overall likelihood* of a threat event is a combination of: (i) the likelihood that the event will occur (e.g., due to human error or natural disaster) or be initiated by an adversary; and (ii) the likelihood that the initiation/occurrence will result in adverse impacts. Organizations assess the overall likelihood of threat events by using inputs from Tables G-2, G-3, and G-4. Any specific algorithm or rule for combining the determined likelihood values depends on: (i) general organizational attitudes toward risk, including overall risk tolerance and tolerance for uncertainty; (ii) specific tolerances toward uncertainty in different risk factors; and (iii) organizational weighting of risk factors. For example, organizations could use any of the following rules (or could define a different rule): (i) use the maximum of the two likelihood values; (ii) use the minimum of the two likelihood values; (iii) consider likelihood of initiation/occurrence only, assuming that if threat events are initiated or occur, the events will result in adverse impacts; (iv) consider likelihood of impact only, assuming that if threat events could result in adverse impacts, adversaries will initiate the events; or (v) take a weighted average of the two likelihood values. Organizations make explicit the rules used.

Appendix G provides a set of exemplary tables for use in determining likelihood of threat events:

- Table G-1 provides a set of exemplary inputs to the likelihood determination task;
- Table G-2 provides an exemplary assessment scale for assessing the likelihood of initiation for adversarial threat events;
- Table G-3 provides an exemplary assessment scale for assessing the likelihood of non-adversarial threat events occurring;
- Table G-4 provides an exemplary assessment scale for assessing the likelihood of threat events having adverse impacts if the events are initiated (adversarial) or occur (non-adversarial); and
- Table G-5 provides an exemplary assessment scale for assessing the overall likelihood of threat events (i.e., a combination of the likelihood of initiation/occurrence and the likelihood of impact).

The information produced in Task 2-4 provides threat event likelihood inputs to the risk tables in Appendix I.

Summary of Key Activities – Task 2-4

- Identify likelihood determination inputs (see **Table G-1**, as tailored by the organization).
- Identify likelihood determination factors using organization-defined information sources (e.g., threat source characteristics, vulnerabilities, predisposing conditions).
- Assess the likelihood of threat event initiation for adversarial threats and the likelihood of threat event occurrence for non-adversarial threats (see **Table G-2** and **Table G-3**, as tailored by the organization).
- Assess the likelihood of threat events resulting in adverse impacts, given likelihood of initiation or occurrence (see **Table G-4**, as tailored by the organization).
- Assess the overall likelihood of threat event initiation/occurrence and likelihood of threat events resulting in adverse impacts (see **Table G-5**, as tailored by the organization).
- Update Columns 7, 10, and 11 in **Table I-5** for adversarial risk (see **Table G-2**, **Table G-4**, and **Table G-5**); or update Columns 5, 8, and 9 in **Table I-7** for non-adversarial risk (see **Table G-3**, **Table G-4**, and **Table G-5**).

DETERMINE IMPACT

TASK 2-5: Determine the adverse impacts from threat events of concern considering: (i) the characteristics of the threat sources that could initiate the events; (ii) the vulnerabilities/predisposing conditions identified; and (iii) the susceptibility reflecting the safeguards/countermeasures planned or implemented to impede such events.

Supplemental Guidance: Organizations describe adverse impacts in terms of the potential harm caused to organizational operations and assets, individuals, other organizations, or the Nation. Where the threat event occurs and whether the effects of the event are contained or spread, influences the severity of the impact. Assessing impact can involve identifying assets or potential targets of threat sources, including information resources (e.g., information, data repositories, information systems, applications, information technologies, communications links), people, and physical resources (e.g., buildings, power supplies), which could be affected by threat events. Organizational impacts are defined and prioritized at Tiers 1 and 2, and communicated to Tier 3 as part of risk framing. At Tier 3, impacts are associated with information system capabilities (e.g., processing, display, communications, storage, and retrieval) and resources (e.g., databases, services, components) that could be compromised.

Appendix H provides a set of exemplary tables for use in determining adverse impacts:

- Table H-1 provides a set of exemplary inputs to the impact determination task;

- Table H-2 provides representative examples of adverse impacts to organizations focusing on harm to organizational operations and assets, individuals, other organizations, and the Nation;

- Table H-3 provides an exemplary assessment scale for assessing the impact of threat events; and

- Table H-4 provides a template for summarizing/documenting adverse impacts.

The information produced in Task 2-5 provides adverse impact inputs to the risk tables in Appendix I.

Summary of Key Activities – Task 2-5

- Identify impact determination inputs (see **Table H-1** as tailored by the organization).

- Identify impact determination factors using organization-defined information sources.

- Identify adverse impacts and affected assets (see **Table H-2**, as tailored by the organization); create or update **Table H-4**.

- Assess the maximum impact associated with the affected assets (see **Table H-3**, as tailored by the organization); update **Table H-4**.

- Update Column 12 in **Table I-5** for adversarial risk; or update Column 10 in **Table I-7** for non-adversarial risk.

DETERMINE RISK

TASK 2-6: Determine the risk to the organization from threat events of concern considering: (i) the impact that would result from the events; and (ii) the likelihood of the events occurring.

Supplemental Guidance: Organizations assess the risks from threat events as a combination of likelihood and impact. The level of risk associated with identified threat events represents a determination of the degree to which organizations are threatened by such events. Organizations make explicit the uncertainty in the risk determinations, including, for example, organizational assumptions and subjective judgments/decisions. Organizations can order the list of threat events of concern by the level of risk determined during the risk assessment—with the greatest attention going to high-risk events. Organizations can further prioritize risks at the same level or with similar scores (see Appendix J). Each risk corresponds to a specific threat event with a level of impact if that event occurs. In general, the risk level is typically not higher than the impact level, and likelihood can serve to reduce risk below that impact level. However, when addressing organization-wide risk management issues with a large number of missions/business functions, mission/business processes, and supporting information systems, impact as an upper bound on risk may not hold. For example, when multiple risks materialize, even if each risk is at the moderate level, the set of those moderate-level risks could aggregate to a higher level of risk for organizations. To address situations where harm occurs multiple times, organizations can define a threat event as multiple occurrences of harm and an impact level associated with the cumulative degree of harm. During the execution of Tasks 2-1 through 2-5, organizations capture key information related to uncertainties in risk assessments. These uncertainties arise from sources such as missing information, subjective determinations, and assumptions made. The effectiveness of risk assessment results is in part determined by the ability of decision makers to be able to determine the continued applicability of assumptions made as part of the assessment. Information related to uncertainty is compiled and presented in a manner that readily supports informed risk management decisions.

Appendix I provides a set of exemplary tables for use in determining risk:

- Table I-1 provides a set of exemplary inputs to the risk and uncertainty determination task;

- Tables I-2 and I-3 provide exemplary assessment scales for assessing levels of risk;

- Tables I-4 and I-6 provide descriptions of column headings for key data elements used in risk determinations for adversarial and non-adversarial threat events, respectively; and

- Tables I-5 and I-7 provide templates for summarizing/documenting key data elements used in risk determinations for adversarial and non-adversarial threat events, respectively.

The information produced in Task 2-6 provides risk inputs to the risk tables in Appendix I.

Summary of Key Activities – Task 2-6

- Identify risk and uncertainty determination inputs (see **Table I-1**, as tailored by the organization).

- Determine risk (see **Table I-2** and **Table I-3**, as tailored by the organization); update Column 13 in **Table I-5** for adversarial risk and Column 11 in **Table I-7** for non-adversarial risk.

3.3 COMMUNICATING AND SHARING RISK ASSESSMENT INFORMATION

The third step in the risk assessment process is to *communicate* the assessment results and *share* risk-related information.[47] The objective of this step is to ensure that decision makers across the organization have the appropriate risk-related information needed to inform and guide risk decisions. Communicating and sharing information consists of the following specific tasks:

- Communicate the risk assessment results; and

- Share information developed in the execution of the risk assessment, to support other risk management activities.

STEP 3: COMMUNICATE AND SHARE RISK ASSESSMENT RESULTS

COMMUNICATE RISK ASSESSMENT RESULTS

TASK 3-1: Communicate risk assessment results to organizational decision makers to support risk responses.

Supplemental Guidance: Organizations can communicate risk assessment results in a variety of ways (e.g., executive briefings, risk assessment reports, dashboards). Such risk communications can be formal or informal with the content and format determined by organizations initiating and conducting the assessments. Organizations provide guidance on specific risk communication and reporting requirements, included as part of preparing for the risk assessment (if not provided in the risk management strategy as part of the risk framing task). Organizations prioritize risks at the same level or with similar scores (see Appendix J). Appendix K provides an example of type of information that may be included in a risk assessment report or the preferred vehicle for risk communication.

SHARE RISK-RELATED INFORMATION

TASK 3-2: Share risk-related information produced during the risk assessment with appropriate organizational personnel.

Supplemental Guidance: Organizations share source information and intermediate results and provide guidance on sharing risk-related information. Information sharing occurs primarily within organizations, via reports and briefings, and by updating risk-related data repositories with supporting evidence for the risk assessment results. Information sharing is also supported by documenting the sources of information, analytical processes, and intermediate results (e.g., the completed tables in Appendices D-I), so that risk assessments can be easily maintained. Information sharing may also occur with other organizations.

> ### *Summary of Key Activities – Communicating and Sharing Information*
>
> - Determine the appropriate method (e.g., executive briefing, risk assessment report, or dashboard) to communicate risk assessment results.
>
> - Communicate risk assessment *results* to designated organizational stakeholders.
>
> - Share the *risk assessment results* and supporting evidence in accordance with organizational policies and guidance.

---

[47] The risk assessment process entails ongoing communications and information sharing between those personnel performing assessment activities, subject matter experts, and key organizational stakeholders (e.g., mission/business owners, risk executive [function], chief information security officers, information system owners/program managers). This communication and information sharing ensures that: (i) the inputs to risk assessments are as accurate as possible; (ii) intermediate results can be used (e.g., to support risk assessments at other tiers); and (iii) results are meaningful and useful inputs to risk response.

3.4   MAINTAINING THE RISK ASSESSMENT

The fourth step in the risk assessment process is to *maintain* the assessment. The objective of this step is to keep current, the specific knowledge of the risk organizations incur. The results of risk assessments inform risk management decisions and guide risk responses. To support the ongoing review of risk management decisions (e.g., acquisition decisions, authorization decisions for information systems and common controls, connection decisions), organizations maintain risk assessments to incorporate any changes detected through risk monitoring.[48] Risk monitoring provides organizations with the means to, on an ongoing basis: (i) determine the *effectiveness* of risk responses; (ii) identify risk-impacting *changes* to organizational information systems and the environments in which those systems operate;[49] and (iii) verify *compliance*.[50] Maintaining risk assessments includes the following specific tasks:

- Monitor risk factors identified in risk assessments on an ongoing basis and understanding subsequent changes to those factors; and

- Update the components of risk assessments reflecting the monitoring activities carried out by organizations.

STEP 4: MAINTAIN THE ASSESSMENT

MONITOR RISK FACTORS

TASK 4-1: Conduct ongoing monitoring of the risk factors that contribute to changes in risk to organizational operations and assets, individuals, other organizations, or the Nation.

Supplemental Guidance: Organizations monitor risk factors of importance on an ongoing basis to ensure that the information needed to make credible, risk-based decisions continues to be available over time. Monitoring risk factors (e.g., threat sources and threat events, vulnerabilities and predisposing conditions, capabilities and intent of adversaries, targeting of organizational operations, assets, or individuals) can provide critical information on changing conditions that could potentially affect the ability of organizations to conduct core missions and business functions. Information derived from the ongoing monitoring of risk factors can be used to refresh risk assessments at whatever frequency deemed appropriate. Organizations can also attempt to capture changes in the effectiveness of risk response measures in order to maintain the currency of risk assessments. The objective is to maintain an ongoing situational awareness of the organizational governance structures and activities, mission/business processes, information systems, and environments of operation, and thereby all of the risk factors that may affect the risk being incurred by organizations. Therefore, in applying the risk assessment context or risk frame (i.e., scope, purpose, assumptions, constraints, risk tolerances, priorities, and trade-offs), organizations consider the part risk factors play in the risk response plan executed. For example, it is expected to be quite common for the security posture of information systems (that is, the risk factors measured within those systems) to reflect only a part of the organizational risk response, with response actions at the organization level or mission/business process level providing a significant portion of that response. In

---

[48] *Risk monitoring*, the fourth step in the risk management process, is described in NIST Special Publication 800-39. The step in the risk assessment process to maintain the assessment results over time overlaps to some degree with the risk monitoring step in the risk management process and the continuous monitoring step in the RMF. This overlap reinforces the important concept that many of the activities in the risk management process are complementary and mutually reinforcing. For example, the continuous monitoring step in the RMF can be used to monitor the ongoing effectiveness of deployed security controls with the results used to inform and guide a more extensive organizational risk monitoring process. At the organization level, risk monitoring may include monitoring key risk factors that are necessary to conduct subsequent risk assessments. Organizations use the risk management strategy to convey key requirements for maintaining risk assessments including, for example, risk factors to monitor and the frequency of such monitoring.

[49] NIST Special Publication 800-137 provides guidance on the ongoing monitoring of organizational information systems and environments of operation.

[50] Compliance verification ensures that organizations have implemented required risk response measures and that information security requirements derived from and traceable to organizational missions/business functions, federal legislation, directives, regulations, policies, and standards/guidelines are satisfied.

such situations, monitoring only the security posture of information systems would likely not provide sufficient information to determine the overall risk being incurred by organizations. Highly capable, well-resourced, and purpose-driven threat sources can be expected to defeat commonly available protection mechanisms (e.g., by bypassing or tampering with such mechanisms). Thus, process-level risk response measures such as reengineering mission/business processes, wise use of information technology, or the use of alternate execution processes, in the event of compromised information systems, can be major elements of organizational risk response plans.

UPDATE RISK ASSESSMENT

TASK 4-2: Update existing risk assessment using the results from ongoing monitoring of risk factors.

Supplemental Guidance: Organizations determine the frequency and the circumstances under which risk assessments are updated. Such determinations can include, for example, the current level of risk to and/or the importance of, core organizational missions/business functions. If significant changes (as defined by organizational policies, direction, or guidance) have occurred since the risk assessment was conducted, organizations can revisit the purpose, scope, assumptions, and constraints of the assessment to determine whether all tasks in the risk assessment process need to be repeated. Otherwise, the updates constitute subsequent risk assessments, identifying and assessing only how selected risk factors have changed, for example: (i) the identification of new threat events, vulnerabilities, predisposing conditions, undesirable consequences and/or affected assets; and (ii) the assessments of threat source characteristics (e.g., capability, intent, targeting, range of effects), likelihoods, and impacts. Organizations communicate the results of subsequent risk assessments to entities across all risk management tiers to ensure that responsible organizational officials have access to critical information needed to make ongoing risk-based decisions.

Summary of Key Activities – Maintaining Risk Assessments

- Identify key **risk factors** that have been identified for ongoing monitoring.
- Identify the **frequency** of risk factor monitoring activities and the **circumstances** under which the risk assessment needs to be updated.
- Reconfirm the **purpose, scope,** and **assumptions** of the risk assessment.
- Conduct the appropriate risk assessment **tasks**, as needed.
- Communicate the subsequent risk assessment **results** to specified organizational personnel.

APPENDIX A

REFERENCES

LAWS, POLICIES, DIRECTIVES, INSTRUCTIONS, STANDARDS, AND GUIDELINES

LEGISLATION

1. E-Government Act [includes FISMA] (P.L. 107-347), December 2002.

2. Federal Information Security Management Act (P.L. 107-347, Title III), December 2002.

POLICIES, DIRECTIVES, INSTRUCTIONS

1. Office of Management and Budget, Circular A-130, Appendix III, Transmittal Memorandum #4, *Management of Federal Information Resources*, November 2000.

2. Committee on National Security Systems Instruction (CNSSI) No. 4009, *National Information Assurance (IA) Glossary*, April 2010.

3. Committee on National Security Systems Instruction (CNSSI) No. 1253, *Security Categorization and Control Selection for National Security Systems*, March 2012.

4. Department of Homeland Security Federal Continuity Directive 2 (FCD 2), *Federal Executive Branch Mission Essential Function and Primary Mission Essential Function Identification and Submission Process*, February 2008.

STANDARDS

1. National Institute of Standards and Technology Federal Information Processing Standards Publication 199, *Standards for Security Categorization of Federal Information and Information Systems*, February 2004.

2. National Institute of Standards and Technology Federal Information Processing Standards Publication 200, *Minimum Security Requirements for Federal Information and Information Systems*, March 2006.

3. ISO/IEC 31000:2009, *Risk management – Principles and guidelines.*

4. ISO/IEC 30101:2009, *Risk management – Risk assessment techniques.*

5. ISO/IEC Guide 73, *Risk management – Vocabulary.*

6. ISO/IEC 27005:2011, *Information technology – Security techniques – Information security risk management.*

GUIDELINES

1. National Institute of Standards and Technology Special Publication 800-18, Revision 1, *Guide for Developing Security Plans for Federal Information Systems*, February 2006.

2. National Institute of Standards and Technology Special Publication 800-34, Revision 1, *Contingency Planning Guide for Federal Information Systems*, May 2010.

3. National Institute of Standards and Technology Special Publication 800-37, Revision 1, *Guide for Applying the Risk Management Framework to Federal Information Systems: A Security Life Cycle Approach*, February 2010.

4. National Institute of Standards and Technology Special Publication 800-39, *Managing Information Security Risk: Organization, Mission, and Information System View*, March 2011.

5. National Institute of Standards and Technology Special Publication 800-53, Revision 3, *Recommended Security Controls for Federal Information Systems and Organizations*, August 2009.

6. National Institute of Standards and Technology Special Publication 800-53A, Revision 1, *Guide for Assessing the Security Controls in Federal Information Systems and Organizations: Building Effective Security Assessment Plans*, June 2010.

7. National Institute of Standards and Technology Special Publication 800-59, *Guideline for Identifying an Information System as a National Security System*, August 2003.

8. National Institute of Standards and Technology Special Publication 800-60, Revision 1, *Guide for Mapping Types of Information and Information Systems to Security Categories*, August 2008.

9. National Institute of Standards and Technology Special Publication 800-64, Revision 2, *Security Considerations in the System Development Life Cycle*, October 2008.

10. National Institute of Standards and Technology Special Publication 800-65, *Integrating IT Security into the Capital Planning and Investment Control Process*, January 2005.

11. National Institute of Standards and Technology Special Publication 800-70, Revision 2, *National Checklist Program for IT Products--Guidelines for Checklist Users and Developers*, February 2011.

12. National Institute of Standards and Technology Special Publication 800-117, Version 1.0, *Guide to Adopting and Using the Security Content Automation Protocol (SCAP)*, July 2010.

13. National Institute of Standards and Technology Special Publication 800-126, *The Technical Specification for the Security Content Automation Protocol (SCAP): SCAP Version 1.0*, November 2009.

14. National Institute of Standards and Technology Special Publication 800-137, *Information Security Continuous Monitoring for Federal Information Systems and Organizations*, September 2011.

APPENDIX B

GLOSSARY

COMMON TERMS AND DEFINITIONS

This appendix provides definitions for security terminology used within Special Publication 800-30. The terms in the glossary are consistent with the terms used in the suite of FISMA-related security standards and guidelines developed by NIST. Unless otherwise stated, all terms used in this publication are also consistent with the definitions contained in the CNSSI No. 4009, *National Information Assurance (IA) Glossary.*

Adequate Security [OMB Circular A-130, Appendix III]	Security commensurate with the risk and magnitude of harm resulting from the loss, misuse, or unauthorized access to or modification of information.
Advanced Persistent Threat [NIST SP 800-39]	An adversary with sophisticated levels of expertise and significant resources, allowing it through the use of multiple different attack vectors (e.g., cyber, physical, and deception), to generate opportunities to achieve its objectives which are typically to establish and extend its presence within the information technology infrastructure of organizations for purposes of continually exfiltrating information and/or to undermine or impede critical aspects of a mission, program, or organization, or place itself in a position to do so in the future; moreover, the advanced persistent threat pursues its objectives repeatedly over an extended period of time, adapting to a defender's efforts to resist it, and with determination to maintain the level of interaction needed to execute its objectives.
Adversary [DHS Risk Lexicon]	Individual, group, organization, or government that conducts or has the intent to conduct detrimental activities.
Agency	See *Executive Agency.*
Analysis Approach	The approach used to define the orientation or starting point of the risk assessment, the level of detail in the assessment, and how risks due to similar threat scenarios are treated.
Assessment	See *Security Control Assessment* or *Risk Assessment.*
Assessment Approach	The approach used to assess risk and its contributing risk factors, including quantitatively, qualitatively, or semi-quantitatively.
Assessor	See *Security Control Assessor* or *Risk Assessor.*
Attack [CNSSI No. 4009]	Any kind of malicious activity that attempts to collect, disrupt, deny, degrade, or destroy information system resources or the information itself.

Authentication [FIPS 200]	Verifying the identity of a user, process, or device, often as a prerequisite to allowing access to resources in an information system.
Authenticity [CNSSI No. 4009]	The property of being genuine and being able to be verified and trusted; confidence in the validity of a transmission, a message, or message originator. See *Authentication*.
Authorization (to operate) [CNSSI No. 4009]	The official management decision given by a senior organizational official to authorize operation of an information system and to explicitly accept the risk to organizational operations (including mission, functions, image, or reputation), organizational assets, individuals, other organizations, and the Nation based on the implementation of an agreed-upon set of security controls.
Authorization Boundary [CNSSI No. 4009]	All components of an information system to be authorized for operation by an authorizing official and excludes separately authorized systems, to which the information system is connected.
Authorizing Official [CNSSI No. 4009]	Senior (federal) official or executive with the authority to formally assume responsibility for operating an information system at an acceptable level of risk to organizational operations (including mission, functions, image, or reputation), organizational assets, individuals, other organizations, and the Nation.
Availability [44 U.S.C., Sec. 3542]	Ensuring timely and reliable access to and use of information.
Chief Information Officer [PL 104-106, Sec. 5125(b)]	Agency official responsible for: (i) Providing advice and other assistance to the head of the executive agency and other senior management personnel of the agency to ensure that information technology is acquired and information resources are managed in a manner that is consistent with laws, Executive Orders, directives, policies, regulations, and priorities established by the head of the agency; (ii) Developing, maintaining, and facilitating the implementation of a sound and integrated information technology architecture for the agency; and (iii) Promoting the effective and efficient design and operation of all major information resources management processes for the agency, including improvements to work processes of the agency.
Chief Information Security Officer	See *Senior Agency Information Security Officer*.
Common Control [NIST SP 800-37]	A security control that is inherited by one or more organizational information systems. See *Security Control Inheritance*.

Common Control Provider [CNSSI No. 4009]	An organizational official responsible for the development, implementation, assessment, and monitoring of common controls (i.e., security controls inherited by information systems).
Compensating Security Control [CNSSI No. 4009]	A management, operational, and/or technical control (i.e., safeguard or countermeasure) employed by an organization in lieu of a recommended security control in the low, moderate, or high baselines that provides equivalent or comparable protection for an information system.
Confidentiality [44 U.S.C., Sec. 3542]	Preserving authorized restrictions on information access and disclosure, including means for protecting personal privacy and proprietary information.
Course of Action [NIST SP 800-39]	A time-phased or situation-dependent combination of risk response measures. See *Risk Response*.
Critical Infrastructure	System and assets, whether physical or virtual, so vital to the United States that the incapacity or destruction of such systems and assets would have a debilitating impact on security, national economic security, national public health or safety, or any combination of those matters.
Critical Infrastructure Sectors [HSPD-7]	Information technology; telecommunications; chemical; transportation systems, including mass transit, aviation, maritime, ground/surface, and rail and pipeline systems; emergency services; and postal and shipping.
Criticality [NIST SP 800-60]	A measure of the degree to which an organization depends on the information or information system for the success of a mission or of a business function.
Cyber Attack [CNSSI No. 4009]	An attack, via cyberspace, targeting an enterprise's use of cyberspace for the purpose of disrupting, disabling, destroying, or maliciously controlling a computing environment/infrastructure; or destroying the integrity of the data or stealing controlled information.
Cyber Security [CNSSI No. 4009]	The ability to protect or defend the use of cyberspace from cyber attacks.
Cyberspace [CNSSI No. 4009]	A global domain within the information environment consisting of the interdependent network of information systems infrastructures including the Internet, telecommunications networks, computer systems, and embedded processors and controllers.

Defense-in-Breadth [CNSSI No. 4009]	A planned, systematic set of multidisciplinary activities that seek to identify, manage, and reduce risk of exploitable vulnerabilities at every stage of the system, network, or subcomponent life cycle (system, network, or product design and development; manufacturing; packaging; assembly; system integration; distribution; operations; maintenance; and retirement).
Defense-in-Depth [CNSSI No. 4009]	Information security strategy integrating people, technology, and operations capabilities to establish variable barriers across multiple layers and missions of the organization.
Enterprise [CNSSI No. 4009]	An organization with a defined mission/goal and a defined boundary, using information systems to execute that mission, and with responsibility for managing its own risks and performance. An enterprise may consist of all or some of the following business aspects: acquisition, program management, financial management (e.g., budgets), human resources, security, and information systems, information and mission management. See *Organization*.
Enterprise Architecture [CNSSI No. 4009]	The description of an enterprise's entire set of information systems: how they are configured, how they are integrated, how they interface to the external environment at the enterprise's boundary, how they are operated to support the enterprise mission, and how they contribute to the enterprise's overall security posture.
Environment of Operation	The physical, technical, and organizational setting in which an information system operates, including but not limited to: missions/business functions; mission/business processes; threat space; vulnerabilities; enterprise and information security architectures; personnel; facilities; supply chain relationships; information technologies; organizational governance and culture; acquisition and procurement processes; organizational policies and procedures; organizational assumptions, constraints, risk tolerance, and priorities/trade-offs).
Executive Agency [41 U.S.C., Sec. 403]	An executive department specified in 5 U.S.C., Sec. 101; a military department specified in 5 U.S.C., Sec. 102; an independent establishment as defined in 5 U.S.C., Sec. 104(1); and a wholly owned Government corporation fully subject to the provisions of 31 U.S.C., Chapter 91.

Fault Tree Analysis	A top-down, deductive failure analysis in which an undesired state of a system (top event) is analyzed using Boolean logic to combine a series of lower-level events.
	An analytical approach whereby an undesired state of a system is specified and the system is then analyzed in the context of its environment of operation to find all realistic ways in which the undesired event (top event) can occur.
Federal Agency	See *Executive Agency*.
Federal Information System [40 U.S.C., Sec. 11331]	An information system used or operated by an executive agency, by a contractor of an executive agency, or by another organization on behalf of an executive agency.
Hybrid Security Control [NIST SP 800-53]	A security control that is implemented in an information system in part as a common control and in part as a system-specific control. See *Common Control* and *System-Specific Security Control*.
Impact Level [CNSSI No. 4009]	The magnitude of harm that can be expected to result from the consequences of unauthorized disclosure of information, unauthorized modification of information, unauthorized destruction of information, or loss of information or information system availability.
Impact Value [CNSSI No. 1253]	The assessed potential impact resulting from a compromise of the confidentiality, integrity, or availability of an information type, expressed as a value of low, moderate, or high.
Industrial Control System [NIST SP 800-39]	An information system used to control industrial processes such as manufacturing, product handling, production, and distribution. Industrial control systems include supervisory control and data acquisition systems used to control geographically dispersed assets, as well as distributed control systems and smaller control systems using programmable logic controllers to control localized processes.
Information [CNSSI No. 4009]	Any communication or representation of knowledge such as facts, data, or opinions in any medium or form, including textual, numerical, graphic, cartographic, narrative, or audiovisual.
[FIPS 199]	An instance of an information type.
Information Owner [CNSSI No. 4009]	Official with statutory or operational authority for specified information and responsibility for establishing the controls for its generation, classification, collection, processing, dissemination, and disposal. See *Information Steward*.
Information Resources [44 U.S.C., Sec. 3502]	Information and related resources, such as personnel, equipment, funds, and information technology.

Information Security [44 U.S.C., Sec. 3542]	The protection of information and information systems from unauthorized access, use, disclosure, disruption, modification, or destruction in order to provide confidentiality, integrity, and availability.
Information Security Architecture [NIST SP 800-39]	A description of the structure and behavior for an enterprise's security processes, information security systems, personnel and organizational sub-units, showing their alignment with the enterprise's mission and strategic plans.
Information Security Program Plan [NIST SP 800-53]	Formal document that provides an overview of the security requirements for an organization-wide information security program and describes the program management controls and common controls in place or planned for meeting those requirements.
Information Security Risk	The risk to organizational operations (including mission, functions, image, reputation), organizational assets, individuals, other organizations, and the Nation due to the potential for unauthorized access, use, disclosure, disruption, modification, or destruction of information and/or information systems. See *Risk*.
Information Steward [CNSSI No. 4009]	An agency official with statutory or operational authority for specified information and responsibility for establishing the controls for its generation, collection, processing, dissemination, and disposal.
Information System [44 U.S.C., Sec. 3502]	A discrete set of information resources organized for the collection, processing, maintenance, use, sharing, dissemination, or disposition of information.
Information System Boundary	See *Authorization Boundary*.
Information System Owner (or Program Manager)	Official responsible for the overall procurement, development, integration, modification, or operation and maintenance of an information system.
Information System Resilience	The ability of an information system to continue to operate while under attack, even if in a degraded or debilitated state, and to rapidly recover operational capabilities for essential functions after a successful attack.
Information System Security Officer	Individual assigned responsibility by the senior agency information security officer, authorizing official, management official, or information system owner for maintaining the appropriate operational security posture for an information system or program.

Information System-Related Security Risk	Risk that arises through the loss of confidentiality, integrity, or availability of information or information systems considering impacts to organizational operations and assets, individuals, other organizations, and the Nation. A subset of *Information Security Risk*. See *Risk*.
Information Technology [40 U.S.C., Sec. 1401]	Any equipment or interconnected system or subsystem of equipment that is used in the automatic acquisition, storage, manipulation, management, movement, control, display, switching, interchange, transmission, or reception of data or information by the executive agency. For purposes of the preceding sentence, equipment is used by an executive agency if the equipment is used by the executive agency directly or is used by a contractor under a contract with the executive agency which: (i) requires the use of such equipment; or (ii) requires the use, to a significant extent, of such equipment in the performance of a service or the furnishing of a product. The term information technology includes computers, ancillary equipment, software, firmware, and similar procedures, services (including support services), and related resources.
Information Type [FIPS 199]	A specific category of information (e.g., privacy, medical, proprietary, financial, investigative, contractor sensitive, security management) defined by an organization or in some instances, by a specific law, Executive Order, directive, policy, or regulation.
Integrity [44 U.S.C., Sec. 3542]	Guarding against improper information modification or destruction, and includes ensuring information non-repudiation and authenticity.
Likelihood of Occurrence [CNSSI No. 4009, adapted]	A weighted factor based on a subjective analysis of the probability that a given threat is capable of exploiting a given vulnerability or a set of vulnerabilities.
Management Controls [FIPS 200]	The security controls (i.e., safeguards or countermeasures) for an information system that focus on the management of risk and the management of information system security.
Mission/Business Segment	Elements of organizations describing mission areas, common/shared business services, and organization-wide services. Mission/business segments can be identified with one or more information systems which collectively support a mission/business process.

National Security System [44 U.S.C., Sec. 3542]	Any information system (including any telecommunications system) used or operated by an agency or by a contractor of an agency, or other organization on behalf of an agency (i) the function, operation, or use of which involves intelligence activities; involves cryptologic activities related to national security; involves command and control of military forces; involves equipment that is an integral part of a weapon or weapons system; or is critical to the direct fulfillment of military or intelligence missions (excluding a system that is to be used for routine administrative and business applications, for example, payroll, finance, logistics, and personnel management applications); or (ii) is protected at all times by procedures established for information that have been specifically authorized under criteria established by an Executive Order or an Act of Congress to be kept classified in the interest of national defense or foreign policy.
Operational Controls [FIPS 200]	The security controls (i.e., safeguards or countermeasures) for an information system that are primarily implemented and executed by people (as opposed to systems).
Organization [FIPS 200, Adapted]	An entity of any size, complexity, or positioning within an organizational structure (e.g., a federal agency or, as appropriate, any of its operational elements). See *Enterprise*.
Plan of Action and Milestones [OMB Memorandum 02-01]	A document that identifies tasks needing to be accomplished. It details resources required to accomplish the elements of the plan, any milestones in meeting the tasks, and scheduled completion dates for the milestones.
Predisposing Condition	A condition that exists within an organization, a mission/business process, enterprise architecture, or information system including its environment of operation, which contributes to (i.e., increases or decreases) the likelihood that one or more threat events, once initiated, will result in undesirable consequences or adverse impact to organizational operations and assets, individuals, other organizations, or the Nation.
Qualitative Assessment [DHS *Risk Lexicon*]	Use of a set of methods, principles, or rules for assessing risk based on nonnumerical categories or levels.
Quantitative Assessment [DHS *Risk Lexicon*]	Use of a set of methods, principles, or rules for assessing risks based on the use of numbers where the meanings and proportionality of values are maintained inside and outside the context of the assessment.
Repeatability	The ability to repeat an assessment in the future, in a manner that is consistent with, and hence comparable to, prior assessments.

Reproducibility	The ability of different experts to produce the same results from the same data.
Residual Risk [CNSSI No. 4009]	Portion of risk remaining after security measures have been applied.
Risk [CNSSI No. 4009]	A measure of the extent to which an entity is threatened by a potential circumstance or event, and typically a function of: (i) the adverse impacts that would arise if the circumstance or event occurs; and (ii) the likelihood of occurrence. See *Information System-Related Security Risk*.
Risk Assessment [NIST SP 800-39]	The process of identifying, estimating, and prioritizing risks to organizational operations (including mission, functions, image, reputation), organizational assets, individuals, other organizations, and the Nation, resulting from the operation of an information system. Part of risk management, incorporates threat and vulnerability analyses, and considers mitigations provided by security controls planned or in place. Synonymous with risk analysis.
Risk Assessment Methodology	A risk assessment process, together with a risk model, assessment approach, and analysis approach.
Risk Assessment Report	The report which contains the results of performing a risk assessment or the formal output from the process of assessing risk.
Risk Assessor	The individual, group, or organization responsible for conducting a risk assessment.
Risk Executive (Function) [CNSSI No. 4009]	An individual or group within an organization that helps to ensure that: (i) security risk-related considerations for individual information systems, to include the authorization decisions for those systems, are viewed from an organization-wide perspective with regard to the overall strategic goals and objectives of the organization in carrying out its missions and business functions; and (ii) managing risk from individual information systems is consistent across the organization, reflects organizational risk tolerance, and is considered along with other organizational risks affecting mission/business success.
Risk Factor	A characteristic used in a risk model as an input to determining the level of risk in a risk assessment.

Risk Management [NIST SP 800-39] [CNSSI No. 4009, adapted]	The program and supporting processes to manage information security risk to organizational operations (including mission, functions, image, reputation), organizational assets, individuals, other organizations, and the Nation, and includes: (i) establishing the context for risk-related activities; (ii) assessing risk; (iii) responding to risk once determined; and (iv) monitoring risk over time.
Risk Mitigation [CNSSI No. 4009]	Prioritizing, evaluating, and implementing the appropriate risk-reducing controls/countermeasures recommended from the risk management process. A subset of *Risk Response*.
Risk Model	A key component of a risk assessment methodology (in addition to assessment approach and analysis approach) that defines key terms and assessable risk factors.
Risk Monitoring [NIST SP 800-39]	Maintaining ongoing awareness of an organization's risk environment, risk management program, and associated activities to support risk decisions.
Risk Response [NIST SP 800-39]	Accepting, avoiding, mitigating, sharing, or transferring risk to organizational operations (i.e., mission, functions, image, or reputation), organizational assets, individuals, other organizations, or the Nation. See *Course of Action*.
Risk Response Measure [NIST SP 800-39]	A specific action taken to respond to an identified risk.
Root Cause Analysis	A principle-based, systems approach for the identification of underlying causes associated with a particular set of risks.
Security Authorization **(to Operate)**	See *Authorization (to operate)*.
Security Categorization	The process of determining the security category for information or an information system. Security categorization methodologies are described in CNSSI No.1253 for national security systems and in FIPS 199 for other than national security systems.
Security Control Assessment [NIST SP 800-39] [CNSSI No. 4009, Adapted]	The testing and/or evaluation of the management, operational, and technical security controls to determine the extent to which the controls are implemented correctly, operating as intended, and producing the desired outcome with respect to meeting the security requirements for an information system or organization.
Security Control Assessor	The individual, group, or organization responsible for conducting a security control assessment.

Security Control Baseline [CNSSI No. 4009]	The set of minimum security controls defined for a low-impact, moderate-impact, or high-impact information system.
[CNSSI No. 1253]	A set of information security controls that has been established through information security strategic planning activities to address one or more specified security categorizations; this set of security controls is intended to be the initial security control set selected for a specific system once that system's security categorization is determined.
Security Control Enhancement [NIST SP 800-39, adapted]	Statement of security capability to: (i) build in additional, but related, functionality to a basic security control; and/or (ii) increase the strength of a basic control.
Security Control Inheritance [CNSSI No. 4009]	A situation in which an information system or application receives protection from security controls (or portions of security controls) that are developed, implemented, assessed, authorized, and monitored by entities other than those responsible for the system or application; entities either internal or external to the organization where the system or application resides. See *Common Control*.
Security Controls [FIPS 199, CNSSI No. 4009]	The management, operational, and technical controls (i.e., safeguards or countermeasures) prescribed for an information system to protect the confidentiality, integrity, and availability of the system and its information.
Security Impact Analysis [NIST SP 800-37]	The analysis conducted by an organizational official to determine the extent to which changes to the information system have affected the security state of the system.
Security Objective [FIPS 199]	Confidentiality, integrity, or availability.
Security Plan [NIST SP 800-18]	Formal document that provides an overview of the security requirements for an information system or an information security program and describes the security controls in place or planned for meeting those requirements. See *System Security Plan* or *Information Security Program Plan*.
Security Policy [CNSSI No. 4009]	A set of criteria for the provision of security services.
Security Posture [CNSSI No. 4009]	The security status of an enterprise's networks, information, and systems based on information assurance resources (e.g., people, hardware, software, policies) and capabilities in place to manage the defense of the enterprise and to react as the situation changes.

Security Requirements
[FIPS 200]

Requirements levied on an information system that are derived from applicable laws, Executive Orders, directives, policies, standards, instructions, regulations, procedures, or organizational mission/business case needs to ensure the confidentiality, integrity, and availability of the information being processed, stored, or transmitted.

Semi-Quantitative Assessment
[Department of Homeland Security (DHS) *Risk Lexicon*]

Use of a set of methods, principles, or rules for assessing risk based on bins, scales, or representative numbers whose values and meanings are not maintained in other contexts.

Senior Agency
Information Security
Officer
[44 U.S.C., Sec. 3544]

Official responsible for carrying out the Chief Information Officer responsibilities under FISMA and serving as the Chief Information Officer's primary liaison to the agency's authorizing officials, information system owners, and information system security officers.

[Note: Organizations subordinate to federal agencies may use the term *Senior Information Security Officer* or *Chief Information Security Officer* to denote individuals filling positions with similar responsibilities to Senior Agency Information Security Officers.]

Senior Information Security
Officer

See *Senior Agency Information Security Officer*.

Sensitivity
[NIST SP 800-60]

A measure of the importance assigned to information by its owner, for the purpose of denoting its need for protection.

Subsystem
[NIST SP 800-39]

A major subdivision or component of an information system consisting of information, information technology, and personnel that performs one or more specific functions.

Supplementation (Security Controls)
[NIST SP 800-39]

The process of adding security controls or control enhancements to a security control baseline from NIST Special Publication 800-53 or CNSSI No. 1253 in order to adequately meet the organization's risk management needs.

System

See *Information System*.

System Security Plan
[NIST SP 800-18]

Formal document that provides an overview of the security requirements for an information system and describes the security controls in place or planned for meeting those requirements.

System-Specific Security Control
[NIST SP 800-37]

A security control for an information system that has not been designated as a common control or the portion of a hybrid control that is to be implemented within an information system.

Tailoring [NIST SP 800-53, CNSSI No. 4009]	The process by which a security control baseline is modified based on: (i) the application of scoping guidance; (ii) the specification of compensating security controls, if needed; and (iii) the specification of organization-defined parameters in the security controls via explicit assignment and selection statements.
Tailored Security Control Baseline [NIST SP 800-39]	A set of security controls resulting from the application of tailoring guidance to the security control baseline. See *Tailoring*.
Technical Controls [FIPS 200]	Security controls (i.e., safeguards or countermeasures) for an information system that are primarily implemented and executed by the information system through mechanisms contained in the hardware, software, or firmware components of the system.
Threat [CNSSI No.4009]	Any circumstance or event with the potential to adversely impact organizational operations (including mission, functions, image, or reputation), organizational assets, individuals, other organizations, or the Nation through an information system via unauthorized access, destruction, disclosure, or modification of information, and/or denial of service.
Threat Assessment [CNSSI No. 4009]	Process of formally evaluating the degree of threat to an information system or enterprise and describing the nature of the threat.
Threat Event	An event or situation that has the potential for causing undesirable consequences or impact.
Threat Scenario	A set of discrete threat events, associated with a specific threat source or multiple threat sources, partially ordered in time. Synonym for *Threat Campaign*.
Threat Shifting	Response from adversaries to perceived safeguards and/or countermeasures (i.e., security controls), in which the adversaries change some characteristic of their intent to do harm in order to avoid and/or overcome those safeguards/countermeasures.
Threat Source [CNSSI No. 4009]	The intent and method targeted at the intentional exploitation of a vulnerability or a situation and method that may accidentally exploit a vulnerability.
Vulnerability [CNSSI No. 4009]	Weakness in an information system, system security procedures, internal controls, or implementation that could be exploited by a threat source.
Vulnerability Assessment [CNSSI No. 4009]	Systematic examination of an information system or product to determine the adequacy of security measures, identify security deficiencies, provide data from which to predict the effectiveness of proposed security measures, and confirm the adequacy of such measures after implementation.

APPENDIX C

ACRONYMS

COMMON ABBREVIATIONS

APT	Advanced Persistent Threat
BCP	Business Continuity Plan
BIA	Business Impact Analysis
CNSS	Committee on National Security Systems
COOP	Continuity of Operations
DoD	Department of Defense
DHS	Department of Homeland Security
DNI	Director of National Intelligence
EA	Enterprise Architecture
FIPS	Federal Information Processing Standards
FISMA	Federal Information Security Management Act
ICS	Industrial Control System
IEC	International Electrotechnical Commission
ISO	International Organization for Standardization
IT	Information Technology
JTF	Joint Task Force
NIST	National Institute of Standards and Technology
NOFORN	Not Releasable to Foreign Nationals
ODNI	Office of the Director of National Intelligence
OMB	Office of Management and Budget
RAR	Risk Assessment Report
RMF	Risk Management Framework
SCAP	Security Content Automation Protocol
SP	Special Publication
TTP	Tactic Technique Procedure
U.S.C.	United States Code

APPENDIX D

THREAT SOURCES

TAXONOMY OF THREATS SOURCES CAPABLE OF INITIATING THREAT EVENTS

This appendix provides: (i) a description of potentially useful inputs to the *threat source* identification task; (ii) an exemplary taxonomy of threat sources by type, description, and risk factors (i.e., characteristics) used to assess the likelihood and/or impact of such threat sources initiating threat events; (iii) an exemplary set of tailorable assessment scales for assessing those risk factors; and (iv) templates for summarizing and documenting the results of the threat source identification Task 2-1. The taxonomy and assessment scales in this appendix can be used by organizations as a starting point with appropriate tailoring to adjust for organization-specific conditions. Tables D-7 and D-8, outputs from Task 2-1, provide relevant inputs to the risk tables in Appendix I.

TABLE D-1: INPUTS – THREAT SOURCE IDENTIFICATION

Description	Provided To		
	Tier 1	Tier 2	Tier 3

From Tier 1: (Organization level)
 	
- Sources of threat information deemed to be credible (e.g., open source and/or classified threat reports, previous risk/threat assessments). **(Section 3.1, Task 1-4)**
- Threat source information and guidance specific to Tier 1 (e.g., threats related to organizational governance, core missions/business functions, management/operational policies, procedures, and structures, external mission/business relationships).
- Taxonomy of threat sources, annotated by the organization, if necessary. **(Table D-2)**
- Characterization of adversarial and non-adversarial threat sources.
  - Assessment scales for assessing adversary capability, intent, and targeting, annotated by the organization, if necessary. **(Table D-3, Table D-4, Table D-5)**
  - Assessment scale for assessing the range of effects, annotated by the organization, if necessary. **(Table D-6)**
- Threat sources identified in previous risk assessments, if appropriate.
	No	Yes	Yes
			if not provided by Tier 2

From Tier 2: (Mission/business process level) - Threat source information and guidance specific to Tier 2 (e.g., threats related to mission/business processes, EA segments, common infrastructure, support services, common controls, and external dependencies). - Mission/business process-specific characterization of adversarial and non-adversarial threat sources.	Yes via RAR	Yes via peer sharing	Yes
From Tier 3: (Information system level) - Threat source information and guidance specific to Tier 3 (e.g., threats related to information systems, information technologies, information system components, applications, networks, environments of operation). - Information system-specific characterization of adversarial and non-adversarial threat sources.	Yes via RAR	Yes via RAR	Yes via peer sharing

TABLE D-2: TAXONOMY OF THREAT SOURCES

Type of Threat Source	Description	Characteristics

ADVERSARIAL
- Individual
  - Outsider
  - Insider
  - Trusted Insider
  - Privileged Insider
- Group
  - Ad hoc
  - Established
- Organization
  - Competitor
  - Supplier
  - Partner
  - Customer
- Nation-State
	Individuals, groups, organizations, or states that seek to exploit the organization's dependence on cyber resources (i.e., information in electronic form, information and communications technologies, and the communications and information-handling capabilities provided by those technologies).	Capability, Intent, Targeting

ACCIDENTAL - User - Privileged User/Administrator	Erroneous actions taken by individuals in the course of executing their everyday responsibilities.	Range of effects

STRUCTURAL
- Information Technology (IT) Equipment
  - Storage
  - Processing
  - Communications
  - Display
  - Sensor
  - Controller
- Environmental Controls
  - Temperature/Humidity Controls
  - Power Supply
- Software
  - Operating System
  - Networking
  - General-Purpose Application
  - Mission-Specific Application
	Failures of equipment, environmental controls, or software due to aging, resource depletion, or other circumstances which exceed expected operating parameters.	Range of effects

ENVIRONMENTAL
- Natural or man-made disaster
  - Fire
  - Flood/Tsunami
  - Windstorm/Tornado
  - Hurricane
  - Earthquake
  - Bombing
  - Overrun
- Unusual Natural Event (e.g., sunspots)
- Infrastructure Failure/Outage
  - Telecommunications
  - Electrical Power
	Natural disasters and failures of critical infrastructures on which the organization depends, but which are outside the control of the organization.
	
	Note: Natural and man-made disasters can also be characterized in terms of their severity and/or duration. However, because the threat source and the threat event are strongly identified, severity and duration can be included in the description of the threat event (e.g., Category 5 hurricane causes extensive damage to the facilities housing mission-critical systems, making those systems unavailable for three weeks).
		Range of effects

TABLE D-3: ASSESSMENT SCALE – CHARACTERISTICS OF ADVERSARY CAPABILITY

Qualitative Values	Semi-Quantitative Values		Description
Very High	96-100	10	The adversary has a very sophisticated level of expertise, is well-resourced, and can generate opportunities to support multiple successful, continuous, and coordinated attacks.
High	80-95	8	The adversary has a sophisticated level of expertise, with significant resources and opportunities to support multiple successful coordinated attacks.
Moderate	21-79	5	The adversary has moderate resources, expertise, and opportunities to support multiple successful attacks.
Low	5-20	2	The adversary has limited resources, expertise, and opportunities to support a successful attack.
Very Low	0-4	0	The adversary has very limited resources, expertise, and opportunities to support a successful attack.

TABLE D-4: ASSESSMENT SCALE – CHARACTERISTICS OF ADVERSARY INTENT

Qualitative Values	Semi-Quantitative Values		Description
Very High	96-100	10	The adversary seeks to undermine, severely impede, or destroy a core mission or business function, program, or enterprise by exploiting a presence in the organization's information systems or infrastructure. The adversary is concerned about disclosure of tradecraft only to the extent that it would impede its ability to complete stated goals.
High	80-95	8	The adversary seeks to undermine/impede critical aspects of a core mission or business function, program, or enterprise, or place itself in a position to do so in the future, by maintaining a presence in the organization's information systems or infrastructure. The adversary is very concerned about minimizing attack detection/disclosure of tradecraft, particularly while preparing for future attacks.
Moderate	21-79	5	The adversary seeks to obtain or modify specific critical or sensitive information or usurp/disrupt the organization's cyber resources by establishing a foothold in the organization's information systems or infrastructure. The adversary is concerned about minimizing attack detection/disclosure of tradecraft, particularly when carrying out attacks over long time periods. The adversary is willing to impede aspects of the organization's missions/business functions to achieve these ends.
Low	5-20	2	The adversary actively seeks to obtain critical or sensitive information or to usurp/disrupt the organization's cyber resources, and does so without concern about attack detection/disclosure of tradecraft.
Very Low	0-4	0	The adversary seeks to usurp, disrupt, or deface the organization's cyber resources, and does so without concern about attack detection/disclosure of tradecraft.

TABLE D-5: ASSESSMENT SCALE – CHARACTERISTICS OF ADVERSARY TARGETING

Qualitative Values	Semi-Quantitative Values		Description
Very High	96-100	10	The adversary analyzes information obtained via reconnaissance and attacks to target persistently a specific organization, enterprise, program, mission or business function, focusing on specific high-value or mission-critical information, resources, supply flows, or functions; specific employees or positions; supporting infrastructure providers/suppliers; or partnering organizations.
High	80-95	8	The adversary analyzes information obtained via reconnaissance to target persistently a specific organization, enterprise, program, mission or business function, focusing on specific high-value or mission-critical information, resources, supply flows, or functions, specific employees supporting those functions, or key positions.
Moderate	21-79	5	The adversary analyzes publicly available information to target persistently specific high-value organizations (and key positions, such as Chief Information Officer), programs, or information.
Low	5-20	2	The adversary uses publicly available information to target a class of high-value organizations or information, and seeks targets of opportunity within that class.
Very Low	0-4	0	The adversary may or may not target any specific organizations or classes of organizations.

TABLE D-6: ASSESSMENT SCALE – RANGE OF EFFECTS FOR NON-ADVERSARIAL THREAT SOURCES

Qualitative Values	Semi-Quantitative Values		Description
Very High	96-100	10	The effects of the error, accident, or act of nature are **sweeping**, involving almost all of the cyber resources of the [Tier 3: information systems; Tier 2: mission/business processes or EA segments, common infrastructure, or support services; Tier 1: organization/governance structure].
High	80-95	8	The effects of the error, accident, or act of nature are **extensive**, involving most of the cyber resources of the [Tier 3: information systems; Tier 2: mission/business processes or EA segments, common infrastructure, or support services; Tier 1: organization/governance structure], including many critical resources.
Moderate	21-79	5	The effects of the error, accident, or act of nature are **wide-ranging**, involving a significant portion of the cyber resources of the [Tier 3: information systems; Tier 2: mission/business processes or EA segments, common infrastructure, or support services; Tier 1: organization/governance structure], including some critical resources.
Low	5-20	2	The effects of the error, accident, or act of nature are **limited**, involving some of the cyber resources of the [Tier 3: information systems; Tier 2: mission/business processes or EA segments, common infrastructure, or support services; Tier 1: organization/governance structure], but involving no critical resources.
Very Low	0-4	0	The effects of the error, accident, or act of nature are **minimal,** involving few if any of the cyber resources of the [Tier 3: information systems; Tier 2: mission/business processes or EA segments, common infrastructure, or support services; Tier 1: organization/governance structure], and involving no critical resources.

TABLE D-7: TEMPLATE – IDENTIFICATION OF ADVERSARIAL THREAT SOURCES

Identifier	Threat Source Source of Information	In Scope	Capability	Intent	Targeting
Organization -defined	Table D-2 and Task 1-4 or Organization-defined	Yes / No	Table D-3 or Organization -defined	Table D-4 or Organization -defined	Table D-5 or Organization -defined

TABLE D-8: TEMPLATE – IDENTIFICATION OF NON-ADVERSARIAL THREAT SOURCES

Identifier	Threat Source Source of Information	In Scope	Range of Effects
Organization -defined	Table D-2 and Task 1-4 or Organization-defined	Yes / No	Table D-6 or Organization-defined

APPENDIX E

THREAT EVENTS
REPRESENTATIVE THREAT EVENTS INITIATED BY THREAT SOURCES

This appendix provides: (i) a description of potentially useful inputs to the *threat event* identification task; (ii) representative examples of adversarial threat events expressed as tactics, techniques, and procedures (TTPs) and non-adversarial threat events; (iii) an exemplary assessment scale for the relevance of those threat events; and (iv) templates for summarizing and documenting the results of the threat identification Task 2-2. Organizations can eliminate certain threat events from further consideration if no adversary with the necessary capability has been identified.[51] Organizations can also modify the threat events provided to describe specific TTPs with sufficient detail[52] and at the appropriate classification level.[53] Organizations can use the representative threat events and predicated/expected values for the relevance of those events as a starting point with tailoring to adjust for any organization-specific conditions. Table E-5, an output from Task 2-2, provides relevant inputs to the risk tables in Appendix I.

TABLE E-1: INPUTS – THREAT EVENT IDENTIFICATION

Description	Provided To		
	Tier 1	Tier 2	Tier 3
From Tier 1: (Organization level) - Sources of threat information deemed to be credible (e.g., open source and/or classified threat reports, previous risk/threat assessments. (**Section 3.1, Task 1-4.**) - Threat event information and guidance specific to Tier 1 (e.g., threats related to organizational governance, core missions/business functions, external mission/business relationships, management/operational policies, procedures, and structures). - Exemplary adversarial threat events, annotated by the organization, if necessary. (**Table E-2**) - Exemplary non-adversarial threat events, annotated by the organization, if necessary. (**Table E-3**) - Assessment scale for assessing the relevance of threat events, annotated by the organization, if necessary. (**Table E-4**) - Threat events identified in previous risk assessments, if appropriate.	No	Yes	Yes If not provided by Tier 2
From Tier 2: (Mission/business process level) - Threat event information and guidance specific to Tier 2 (e.g., threats related to mission/business processes, EA segments, common infrastructure, support services, common controls, and external dependencies). - Mission/business process-specific characterization of adversarial and non-adversarial threat events.	Yes Via RAR	Yes Via Peer Sharing	Yes
From Tier 3: (Information system level) - Threat event information and guidance specific to Tier 3 (e.g., threats related to information systems, information technologies, information system components, applications, networks, environments of operation). - Information system-specific characterization of adversarial and non-adversarial threat events. - Incident reports.	Yes Via RAR	Yes Via RAR	Yes Via Peer Sharing

[51] Each entry in Table E-2 implicitly assumes a level of adversary capability, intent, and targeting. Depending on the results of threat source identification, some entries could be determined to be irrelevant, while other entries could be combined. In addition, some entries could be rewritten in terms of an organization's enterprise architecture.

[52] The level of detail of TTPs is established as part of the organizational risk frame. The level of detail in Table E-2 is intended to support risk assessments at all three tiers, and to be tailorable to include additional details, as necessary. More detailed descriptions of threat events that exploit software, for example, can be found in the Common Attack Pattern Enumeration and Classification (CAPEC) site at http://capec.mitre.org.

[53] The threat events in Table E-2 are provided at the *unclassified* level. Additional threat events at the *classified* level are available from selected federal agencies to individuals with appropriate security clearances and need to know.

TABLE E-2: REPRESENTATIVE EXAMPLES – ADVERSARIAL THREAT EVENTS[54]

Threat Events (Characterized by TTPs)	Description
Perform reconnaissance and gather information.	
Perform perimeter network reconnaissance/scanning.	Adversary uses commercial or free software to scan organizational perimeters to obtain a better understanding of the information technology infrastructure and improve the ability to launch successful attacks.
Perform network sniffing of exposed networks.	Adversary with access to exposed wired or wireless data channels used to transmit information, uses network sniffing to identify components, resources, and protections.
Gather information using open source discovery of organizational information.	Adversary mines publically accessible information to gather information about organizational information systems, business processes, users or personnel, or external relationships that the adversary can subsequently employ in support of an attack.
Perform reconnaissance and surveillance of targeted organizations.	Adversary uses various means (e.g., scanning, physical observation) over time to examine and assess organizations and ascertain points of vulnerability.
Perform malware-directed internal reconnaissance.	Adversary uses malware installed inside the organizational perimeter to identify targets of opportunity. Because the scanning, probing, or observation does not cross the perimeter, it is not detected by externally placed intrusion detection systems.
Craft or create attack tools.	
Craft phishing attacks.	Adversary counterfeits communications from a legitimate/trustworthy source to acquire sensitive information such as usernames, passwords, or SSNs. Typical attacks occur via email, instant messaging, or comparable means; commonly directing users to websites that appear to be legitimate sites, while actually stealing the entered information.
Craft spear phishing attacks.	Adversary employs phishing attacks targeted at high value targets (e.g., senior leaders/executives).
Craft attacks specifically based on deployed information technology environment.	Adversary develops attacks (e.g., crafts targeted malware) that take advantage of adversary knowledge of the organizational information technology environment.
Create counterfeit/spoof website.	Adversary creates duplicates of legitimate websites; when users visit a counterfeit site, the site can gather information or download malware.
Craft counterfeit certificates.	Adversary counterfeits or compromises a certificate authority, so that malware or connections will appear legitimate.
Create and operate false front organizations to inject malicious components into the supply chain.	Adversary creates false front organizations with the appearance of legitimate suppliers in the critical life-cycle path that then inject corrupted/malicious information system components into the organizational supply chain.
Deliver/insert/install malicious capabilities.	
Deliver known malware to internal organizational information systems (e.g., virus via email).	Adversary uses common delivery mechanisms (e.g., email) to install/insert known malware (e. g., malware whose existence is known) into organizational information systems.
Deliver modified malware to internal organizational information systems.	Adversary uses more sophisticated delivery mechanisms than email (e.g., web traffic, instant messaging, FTP) to deliver malware and possibly modifications of known malware to gain access to internal organizational information systems.
Deliver targeted malware for control of internal systems and exfiltration of data.	Adversary installs malware that is specifically designed to take control of internal organizational information systems, identify sensitive information, exfiltrate the information back to adversary, and conceal these actions.
Deliver malware by providing removable media.	Adversary places removable media (e.g., flash drives) containing malware in locations external to organizational physical perimeters but where employees are likely to find the media (e.g., facilities parking lots, exhibits at conferences attended by employees) and use it on organizational information systems.

---

[54] While not restricted to the APT as a threat source, the threat events in Table E-2 generally follow the flow of an APT campaign. Within each stage in a campaign, similar events are listed in order of adversary capability.

Threat Events (Characterized by TTPs)	Description
Insert untargeted malware into downloadable software and/or into commercial information technology products.	Adversary corrupts or inserts malware into common freeware, shareware or commercial information technology products. Adversary is not targeting specific organizations, simply looking for entry points into internal organizational information systems. Note that this is particularly a concern for mobile applications.
Insert targeted malware into organizational information systems and information system components.	Adversary inserts malware into organizational information systems and information system components (e.g., commercial information technology products), specifically targeted to the hardware, software, and firmware used by organizations (based on knowledge gained via reconnaissance).
Insert specialized malware into organizational information systems based on system configurations.	Adversary inserts specialized, non-detectable, malware into organizational information systems based on system configurations, specifically targeting critical information system components based on reconnaissance and placement within organizational information systems.
Insert counterfeit or tampered hardware into the supply chain.	Adversary intercepts hardware from legitimate suppliers. Adversary modifies the hardware or replaces it with faulty or otherwise modified hardware.
Insert tampered critical components into organizational systems.	Adversary replaces, though supply chain, subverted insider, or some combination thereof, critical information system components with modified or corrupted components.
Install general-purpose sniffers on organization-controlled information systems or networks.	Adversary installs sniffing software onto internal organizational information systems or networks.
Install persistent and targeted sniffers on organizational information systems and networks.	Adversary places within internal organizational information systems or networks software designed to (over a continuous period of time) collect (sniff) network traffic.
Insert malicious scanning devices (e.g., wireless sniffers) inside facilities.	Adversary uses postal service or other commercial delivery services to deliver to organizational mailrooms a device that is able to scan wireless communications accessible from within the mailrooms and then wirelessly transmit information back to adversary.
Insert subverted individuals into organizations.	Adversary places individuals within organizations who are willing and able to carry out actions to cause harm to organizational missions/business functions.
Insert subverted individuals into privileged positions in organizations.	Adversary places individuals in privileged positions within organizations who are willing and able to carry out actions to cause harm to organizational missions/business functions. Adversary may target privileged functions to gain access to sensitive information (e.g., user accounts, system files, etc.) and may leverage access to one privileged capability to get to another capability.
Exploit and compromise.	
Exploit physical access of authorized staff to gain access to organizational facilities.	Adversary follows ("tailgates") authorized individuals into secure/controlled locations with the goal of gaining access to facilities, circumventing physical security checks.
Exploit poorly configured or unauthorized information systems exposed to the Internet.	Adversary gains access through the Internet to information systems that are not authorized for Internet connectivity or that do not meet organizational configuration requirements.
Exploit split tunneling.	Adversary takes advantage of external organizational or personal information systems (e.g., laptop computers at remote locations) that are simultaneously connected securely to organizational information systems or networks and to nonsecure remote connections.
Exploit multi-tenancy in a cloud environment.	Adversary, with processes running in an organizationally-used cloud environment, takes advantage of multi-tenancy to observe behavior of organizational processes, acquire organizational information, or interfere with the timely or correct functioning of organizational processes.
Exploit known vulnerabilities in mobile systems (e.g., laptops, PDAs, smart phones).	Adversary takes advantage of fact that transportable information systems are outside physical protection of organizations and logical protection of corporate firewalls, and compromises the systems based on known vulnerabilities to gather information from those systems.
Exploit recently discovered vulnerabilities.	Adversary exploits recently discovered vulnerabilities in organizational information systems in an attempt to compromise the systems before mitigation measures are available or in place.

Threat Events (Characterized by TTPs)	Description
Exploit vulnerabilities on internal organizational information systems.	Adversary searches for known vulnerabilities in organizational internal information systems and exploits those vulnerabilities.
Exploit vulnerabilities using zero-day attacks.	Adversary employs attacks that exploit as yet unpublicized vulnerabilities. Zero-day attacks are based on adversary insight into the information systems and applications used by organizations as well as adversary reconnaissance of organizations.
Exploit vulnerabilities in information systems timed with organizational mission/business operations tempo.	Adversary launches attacks on organizations in a time and manner consistent with organizational needs to conduct mission/business operations.
Exploit insecure or incomplete data deletion in multi-tenant environment.	Adversary obtains unauthorized information due to insecure or incomplete data deletion in a multi-tenant environment (e.g., in a cloud computing environment).
Violate isolation in multi-tenant environment.	Adversary circumvents or defeats isolation mechanisms in a multi-tenant environment (e.g., in a cloud computing environment) to observe, corrupt, or deny service to hosted services and information/data.
Compromise critical information systems via physical access.	Adversary obtains physical access to organizational information systems and makes modifications.
Compromise information systems or devices used externally and reintroduced into the enterprise.	Adversary installs malware on information systems or devices while the systems/devices are external to organizations for purposes of subsequently infecting organizations when reconnected.
Compromise software of organizational critical information systems.	Adversary inserts malware or otherwise corrupts critical internal organizational information systems.
Compromise organizational information systems to facilitate exfiltration of data/information.	Adversary implants malware into internal organizational information systems, where the malware over time can identify and then exfiltrate valuable information.
Compromise mission-critical information.	Adversary compromises the integrity of mission-critical information, thus preventing or impeding ability of organizations to which information is supplied, from carrying out operations.
Compromise design, manufacture, and/or distribution of information system components (including hardware, software, and firmware).	Adversary compromises the design, manufacture, and/or distribution of critical information system components at selected suppliers.
Conduct an attack (i.e., direct/coordinate attack tools or activities).	
Conduct communications interception attacks.	Adversary takes advantage of communications that are either unencrypted or use weak encryption (e.g., encryption containing publically known flaws), targets those communications, and gains access to transmitted information and channels.
Conduct wireless jamming attacks.	Adversary takes measures to interfere with wireless communications so as to impede or prevent communications from reaching intended recipients.
Conduct attacks using unauthorized ports, protocols and services.	Adversary conducts attacks using ports, protocols, and services for ingress and egress that are not authorized for use by organizations.
Conduct attacks leveraging traffic/data movement allowed across perimeter.	Adversary makes use of permitted information flows (e.g., email communication, removable storage) to compromise internal information systems, which allows adversary to obtain and exfiltrate sensitive information through perimeters.
Conduct simple Denial of Service (DoS) attack.	Adversary attempts to make an Internet-accessible resource unavailable to intended users, or prevent the resource from functioning efficiently or at all, temporarily or indefinitely.
Conduct Distributed Denial of Service (DDoS) attacks.	Adversary uses multiple compromised information systems to attack a single target, thereby causing denial of service for users of the targeted information systems.
Conduct targeted Denial of Service (DoS) attacks.	Adversary targets DoS attacks to critical information systems, components, or supporting infrastructures, based on adversary knowledge of dependencies.
Conduct physical attacks on organizational facilities.	Adversary conducts a physical attack on organizational facilities (e.g., sets a fire).
Conduct physical attacks on infrastructures supporting organizational facilities.	Adversary conducts a physical attack on one or more infrastructures supporting organizational facilities (e.g., breaks a water main, cuts a power line).
Conduct cyber-physical attacks on organizational facilities.	Adversary conducts a cyber-physical attack on organizational facilities (e.g., remotely changes HVAC settings).

Threat Events (Characterized by TTPs)	Description
Conduct data scavenging attacks in a cloud environment.	Adversary obtains data used and then deleted by organizational processes running in a cloud environment.
Conduct brute force login attempts/password guessing attacks.	Adversary attempts to gain access to organizational information systems by random or systematic guessing of passwords, possibly supported by password cracking utilities.
Conduct nontargeted zero-day attacks.	Adversary employs attacks that exploit as yet unpublicized vulnerabilities. Attacks are not based on any adversary insights into specific vulnerabilities of organizations.
Conduct externally-based session hijacking.	Adversary takes control of (hijacks) already established, legitimate information system sessions between organizations and external entities (e.g., users connecting from off-site locations).
Conduct internally-based session hijacking.	Adversary places an entity within organizations in order to gain access to organizational information systems or networks for the express purpose of taking control (hijacking) an already established, legitimate session either between organizations and external entities (e.g., users connecting from remote locations) or between two locations within internal networks.
Conduct externally-based network traffic modification (man in the middle) attacks.	Adversary, operating outside organizational systems, intercepts/eavesdrops on sessions between organizational and external systems. Adversary then relays messages between organizational and external systems, making them believe that they are talking directly to each other over a private connection, when in fact the entire communication is controlled by the adversary. Such attacks are of particular concern for organizational use of community, hybrid, and public clouds.
Conduct internally-based network traffic modification (man in the middle) attacks.	Adversary operating within the organizational infrastructure intercepts and corrupts data sessions.
Conduct outsider-based social engineering to obtain information.	Externally placed adversary takes actions (e.g., using email, phone) with the intent of persuading or otherwise tricking individuals within organizations into revealing critical/sensitive information (e.g., personally identifiable information).
Conduct insider-based social engineering to obtain information.	Internally placed adversary takes actions (e.g., using email, phone) so that individuals within organizations reveal critical/sensitive information (e.g., mission information).
Conduct attacks targeting and compromising personal devices of critical employees.	Adversary targets key organizational employees by placing malware on their personally owned information systems and devices (e.g., laptop/notebook computers, personal digital assistants, smart phones). The intent is to take advantage of any instances where employees use personal information systems or devices to handle critical/sensitive information.
Conduct supply chain attacks targeting and exploiting critical hardware, software, or firmware.	Adversary targets and compromises the operation of software (e.g., through malware injections), firmware, and hardware that performs critical functions for organizations. This is largely accomplished as supply chain attacks on both commercial off-the-shelf and custom information systems and components.
Achieve results (i.e., cause adverse impacts, obtain information)	
Obtain sensitive information through network sniffing of external networks.	Adversary with access to exposed wired or wireless data channels that organizations (or organizational personnel) use to transmit information (e.g., kiosks, public wireless networks) intercepts communications.
Obtain sensitive information via exfiltration.	Adversary directs malware on organizational systems to locate and surreptitiously transmit sensitive information.
Cause degradation or denial of attacker-selected services or capabilities.	Adversary directs malware on organizational systems to impair the correct and timely support of organizational mission/business functions.
Cause deterioration/destruction of critical information system components and functions.	Adversary destroys or causes deterioration of critical information system components to impede or eliminate organizational ability to carry out missions or business functions. Detection of this action is not a concern.
Cause integrity loss by creating, deleting, and/or modifying data on publicly accessible information systems (e.g., web defacement).	Adversary vandalizes, or otherwise makes unauthorized changes to, organizational websites or data on websites.
Cause integrity loss by polluting or corrupting critical data.	Adversary implants corrupted and incorrect data in critical data, resulting in suboptimal actions or loss of confidence in organizational data/services.

Threat Events (Characterized by TTPs)	Description
Cause integrity loss by injecting false but believable data into organizational information systems.	Adversary injects false but believable data into organizational information systems, resulting in suboptimal actions or loss of confidence in organizational data/services.
Cause disclosure of critical and/or sensitive information by authorized users.	Adversary induces (e.g., via social engineering) authorized users to inadvertently expose, disclose, or mishandle critical/sensitive information.
Cause unauthorized disclosure and/or unavailability by spilling sensitive information.	Adversary contaminates organizational information systems (including devices and networks) by causing them to handle information of a classification/sensitivity for which they have not been authorized. The information is exposed to individuals who are not authorized access to such information, and the information system, device, or network is unavailable while the spill is investigated and mitigated.
Obtain information by externally located interception of wireless network traffic.	Adversary intercepts organizational communications over wireless networks. Examples include targeting public wireless access or hotel networking connections, and drive-by subversion of home or organizational wireless routers.
Obtain unauthorized access.	Adversary with authorized access to organizational information systems, gains access to resources that exceeds authorization.
Obtain sensitive data/information from publicly accessible information systems.	Adversary scans or mines information on publically accessible servers and web pages of organizations with the intent of finding sensitive information.
Obtain information by opportunistically stealing or scavenging information systems/components.	Adversary steals information systems or components (e. g., laptop computers or data storage media) that are left unattended outside of the physical perimeters of organizations, or scavenges discarded components.
Maintain a presence or set of capabilities.	
Obfuscate adversary actions.	Adversary takes actions to inhibit the effectiveness of the intrusion detection systems or auditing capabilities within organizations.
Adapt cyber attacks based on detailed surveillance.	Adversary adapts behavior in response to surveillance and organizational security measures.
Coordinate a campaign.	
Coordinate a campaign of multi-staged attacks (e.g., hopping).	Adversary moves the source of malicious commands or actions from one compromised information system to another, making analysis difficult.
Coordinate a campaign that combines internal and external attacks across multiple information systems and information technologies.	Adversary combines attacks that require both physical presence within organizational facilities and cyber methods to achieve success. Physical attack steps may be as simple as convincing maintenance personnel to leave doors or cabinets open.
Coordinate campaigns across multiple organizations to acquire specific information or achieve desired outcome.	Adversary does not limit planning to the targeting of one organization. Adversary observes multiple organizations to acquire necessary information on targets of interest.
Coordinate a campaign that spreads attacks across organizational systems from existing presence.	Adversary uses existing presence within organizational systems to extend the adversary's span of control to other organizational systems including organizational infrastructure. Adversary thus is in position to further undermine organizational ability to carry out missions/business functions.
Coordinate a campaign of continuous, adaptive, and changing cyber attacks based on detailed surveillance.	Adversary attacks continually change in response to surveillance and organizational security measures.
Coordinate cyber attacks using external (outsider), internal (insider), and supply chain (supplier) attack vectors.	Adversary employs continuous, coordinated attacks, potentially using all three attack vectors for the purpose of impeding organizational operations.

TABLE E-3: REPRESENTATIVE EXAMPLES – NON-ADVERSARIAL THREAT EVENTS

Threat Event	Description
Spill sensitive information	Authorized user erroneously contaminates a device, information system, or network by placing on it or sending to it information of a classification/sensitivity which it has not been authorized to handle. The information is exposed to access by unauthorized individuals, and as a result, the device, system, or network is unavailable while the spill is investigated and mitigated.
Mishandling of critical and/or sensitive information by authorized users	Authorized privileged user inadvertently exposes critical/sensitive information.
Incorrect privilege settings	Authorized privileged user or administrator erroneously assigns a user exceptional privileges or sets privilege requirements on a resource too low.
Communications contention	Degraded communications performance due to contention.
Unreadable display	Display unreadable due to aging equipment.
Earthquake at primary facility	Earthquake of organization-defined magnitude at primary facility makes facility inoperable.
Fire at primary facility	Fire (not due to adversarial activity) at primary facility makes facility inoperable.
Fire at backup facility	Fire (not due to adversarial activity) at backup facility makes facility inoperable or destroys backups of software, configurations, data, and/or logs.
Flood at primary facility	Flood (not due to adversarial activity) at primary facility makes facility inoperable.
Flood at backup facility	Flood (not due to adversarial activity) at backup facility makes facility inoperable or destroys backups of software, configurations, data, and/or logs.
Hurricane at primary facility	Hurricane of organization-defined strength at primary facility makes facility inoperable.
Hurricane at backup facility	Hurricane of organization-defined strength at backup facility makes facility inoperable or destroys backups of software, configurations, data, and/or logs.
Resource depletion	Degraded processing performance due to resource depletion.
Introduction of vulnerabilities into software products	Due to inherent weaknesses in programming languages and software development environments, errors and vulnerabilities are introduced into commonly used software products.
Disk error	Corrupted storage due to a disk error.
Pervasive disk error	Multiple disk errors due to aging of a set of devices all acquired at the same time, from the same supplier.
Windstorm/tornado at primary facility	Windstorm/tornado of organization-defined strength at primary facility makes facility inoperable.
Windstorm/tornado at backup facility	Windstorm/tornado of organization-defined strength at backup facility makes facility inoperable or destroys backups of software, configurations, data, and/or logs.

TABLE E-4: RELEVANCE OF THREAT EVENTS

Value	Description
Confirmed	The threat event or TTP has been seen by the organization.
Expected	The threat event or TTP has been seen by the organization's peers or partners.
Anticipated	The threat event or TTP has been reported by a trusted source.
Predicted	The threat event or TTP has been predicted by a trusted source.
Possible	The threat event or TTP has been described by a somewhat credible source.
N/A	The threat event or TTP is not currently applicable. For example, a threat event or TTP could assume specific technologies, architectures, or processes that are not present in the organization, mission/business process, EA segment, or information system; or predisposing conditions that are not present (e.g., location in a flood plain). Alternately, if the organization is using detailed or specific threat information, a threat event or TTP could be deemed inapplicable because information indicates that no adversary is expected to initiate the threat event or use the TTP.

TABLE E-5: TEMPLATE – IDENTIFICATION OF THREAT EVENTS

Identifier	Threat Event Source of Information	Threat Source	Relevance
Organization-defined	Table E-2, Table E-3, Task 1-4 or Organization-defined	Table D-7, Table D-8 or Organization-defined	Table E-4 or Organization-defined

APPENDIX F

VULNERABILITIES AND PREDISPOSING CONDITIONS
RISK FACTORS AFFECTING THE LIKELIHOOD OF SUCCESSFUL THREAT EXPLOITATION

This appendix provides: (i) a description of potentially useful inputs to the *vulnerability* and *predisposing condition* identification task; (ii) an exemplary taxonomy of predisposing conditions; (iii) exemplary assessment scales for assessing the severity of vulnerabilities and the pervasiveness of predisposing conditions; and (iv) a set of templates for summarizing and documenting the results of the vulnerability and predisposing condition identification task. The taxonomy and assessment scales in this appendix can be used by organizations as a starting point with appropriate tailoring to adjust for any organization-specific conditions. Tables F-3 and F-6, outputs from Task 2-3, provide relevant inputs to the risk tables in Appendix I.

TABLE F-1: INPUTS – VULNERABILITIES AND PREDISPOSING CONDITIONS

Description	Provided To		
	Tier 1	Tier 2	Tier 3

From Tier 1 (Organization level)
- Sources of vulnerability information deemed to be credible (e.g., open source and/or classified vulnerabilities, previous risk/vulnerability assessments, Mission and/or Business Impact Analyses). **(Section 3.1, Task 1-4.)**
- Vulnerability information and guidance specific to Tier 1 (e.g., vulnerabilities related to organizational governance, core missions/business functions, management/operational policies, procedures, and structures, external mission/business relationships).
- Taxonomy of predisposing conditions, annotated by the organization, if necessary. **(Table F-4)**
- Characterization of vulnerabilities and predisposing conditions.
  - Assessment scale for assessing the severity of vulnerabilities, annotated by the organization, if necessary. **(Table F-2)**
  - Assessment scale for assessing the pervasiveness of predisposing conditions, annotated by the organization, if necessary. **(Table F-5)**
  - Business Continuity Plan, Continuity of Operations Plan for the organization, if such plans are defined for the entire organization.
	No	Yes	Yes
			If not provided by Tier 2

From Tier 2: (Mission/business process level) - Vulnerability information and guidance specific to Tier 2 (e.g., vulnerabilities related to organizational mission/business processes, EA segments, common infrastructure, support services, common controls, and external dependencies). - Business Continuity Plans, Continuity of Operations Plans for mission/business processes, if such plans are defined for individual processes or business units.	Yes Via RAR	Yes Via Peer Sharing	Yes
From Tier 3: (Information system level) - Vulnerability information and guidance specific to Tier 3 (e.g., vulnerabilities related to information systems, information technologies, information system components, applications, networks, environments of operation). - Security assessment reports (i.e., deficiencies in assessed controls identified as vulnerabilities). - Results of monitoring activities (e.g., automated and nonautomated data feeds). - Vulnerability assessments, Red Team reports, or other reports from analyses of information systems, subsystems, information technology products, devices, networks, or applications. - Contingency Plans, Disaster Recovery Plans, Incident Reports. - Vendor/manufacturer vulnerability reports.	Yes Via RAR	Yes Via RAR	Yes Via Peer Sharing

TABLE F-2: ASSESSMENT SCALE – VULNERABILITY SEVERITY

Qualitative Values	Semi-Quantitative Values		Description
Very High	96-100	10	The vulnerability is exposed and exploitable, and its exploitation could result in severe impacts. Relevant security control or other remediation is not implemented and not planned; or no security measure can be identified to remediate the vulnerability.
High	80-95	8	The vulnerability is of high concern, based on the exposure of the vulnerability and ease of exploitation and/or on the severity of impacts that could result from its exploitation. Relevant security control or other remediation is planned but not implemented; compensating controls are in place and at least minimally effective.
Moderate	21-79	5	The vulnerability is of moderate concern, based on the exposure of the vulnerability and ease of exploitation and/or on the severity of impacts that could result from its exploitation. Relevant security control or other remediation is partially implemented and somewhat effective.
Low	5-20	2	The vulnerability is of minor concern, but effectiveness of remediation could be improved. Relevant security control or other remediation is fully implemented and somewhat effective.
Very Low	0-4	0	The vulnerability is not of concern. Relevant security control or other remediation is fully implemented, assessed, and effective.

TABLE F-3: TEMPLATE – IDENTIFICATION OF VULNERABILITIES

Identifier	Vulnerability Source of Information	Vulnerability Severity
Organization-defined	Task 2-3, Task 1-4 or Organization-defined	Table F-2 or Organization-defined

TABLE F-4: TAXONOMY OF PREDISPOSING CONDITIONS

Type of Predisposing Condition	Description

INFORMATION-RELATED
- Classified National Security Information
- Compartments
- Controlled Unclassified Information
- Personally Identifiable Information
- Special Access Programs
- Agreement-Determined
  - NOFORN
  - Proprietary
	Needs to handle information (as it is created, transmitted, stored, processed, and/or displayed) in a specific manner, due to its sensitivity (or lack of sensitivity), legal or regulatory requirements, and/or contractual or other organizational agreements.

TECHNICAL
- Architectural
  - Compliance with technical standards
  - Use of specific products or product lines
  - Solutions for and/or approaches to user-based collaboration and information sharing
  - Allocation of specific security functionality to common controls
- Functional
  - Networked multiuser
  - Single-user
  - Stand-alone / nonnetworked
  - Restricted functionality (e.g., communications, sensors, embedded controllers)
	Needs to use technologies in specific ways.

OPERATIONAL / ENVIRONMENTAL
- Mobility
  - Fixed-site (specify location)
  - Semi-mobile
    - Land-based, Airborne, Sea-based, Space-based
  - Mobile (e.g., handheld device)
- Population with physical and/or logical access to components of the information system, mission/business process, EA segment
  - Size of population
  - Clearance/vetting of population
	Ability to rely upon physical, procedural, and personnel controls provided by the operational environment.

TABLE F-5: ASSESSMENT SCALE – PERVASIVENESS OF PREDISPOSING CONDITIONS

Qualitative Values	Semi-Quantitative Values		Description
Very High	96-100	10	Applies to **all** organizational missions/business functions (Tier 1), mission/business processes (Tier 2), or information systems (Tier 3).
High	80-95	8	Applies to **most** organizational missions/business functions (Tier 1), mission/business processes (Tier 2), or information systems (Tier 3).
Moderate	21-79	5	Applies to **many** organizational missions/business functions (Tier 1), mission/business processes (Tier 2), or information systems (Tier 3).
Low	5-20	2	Applies to **some** organizational missions/business functions (Tier 1), mission/business processes (Tier 2), or information systems (Tier 3).
Very Low	0-4	0	Applies to **few** organizational missions/business functions (Tier 1), mission/business processes (Tier 2), or information systems (Tier 3).

TABLE F-6: TEMPLATE – IDENTIFICATION OF PREDISPOSING CONDITIONS

Identifier	Predisposing Condition Source of Information	Pervasiveness of Condition
Organization-defined	Table F-4, Task 1-4 or Organization-defined	Table F-5 or Organization-defined

APPENDIX G

LIKELIHOOD OF OCCURRENCE

DETERMINING THE LIKELIHOOD OF THREAT EVENTS CAUSING ADVERSE IMPACTS

This appendix provides: (i) a description of potentially useful inputs to the *likelihood*[55] determination task; and (ii) exemplary assessment scales for assessing the likelihood of threat event initiation/occurrence, the likelihood of threat events resulting in adverse impacts, and the overall likelihood of threat events being initiated or occurring and doing damage to organizational operations, assets, or individuals. The assessment scales in this appendix can be used by organizations as a starting point with appropriate tailoring to adjust for any organization-specific conditions. Tables G-2, G-3, G-4, and G-5, outputs from Task 2-4, provide relevant inputs to the risk tables in Appendix I.

TABLE G-1: INPUTS – DETERMINATION OF LIKELIHOOD

Description	Provided To		
	Tier 1	Tier 2	Tier 3
From Tier 1 (Organization level) - Likelihood information and guidance specific to Tier 1 (e.g., likelihood information related to organizational governance, core missions/business functions, management/operational policies, procedures, and structures, external mission/business relationships). - Guidance on organization-wide levels of likelihood needing no further consideration. - Assessment scale for assessing the likelihood of threat event initiation (adversarial threat events), annotated by the organization, if necessary. **(Table G-2)** - Assessment scale for assessing the likelihood of threat event occurrence (non-adversarial threat events), annotated by the organization, if necessary. **(Table G-3)** - Assessment scale for assessing the likelihood of threat events resulting in adverse impacts, annotated by the organization, if necessary. **(Table G-4)** - Assessment scale for assessing the overall likelihood of threat events being initiated or occurring and resulting in adverse impacts, annotated by the organization, if necessary. **(Table G-5)**	No	Yes	Yes If not provided by Tier 2
From Tier 2: (Mission/business process level) - Likelihood information and guidance specific to Tier 2 (e.g., likelihood information related to mission/business processes, EA segments, common infrastructure, support services, common controls, and external dependencies).	Yes Via RAR	Yes Via Peer Sharing	Yes
From Tier 3: (Information system level) - Likelihood information and guidance specific to Tier 3 (e.g., likelihood information related to information systems, information technologies, information system components, applications, networks, environments of operation). - Historical data on successful and unsuccessful cyber attacks; attack detection rates. - Security assessment reports (i.e., deficiencies in assessed controls identified as vulnerabilities). - Results of monitoring activities (e.g., automated and nonautomated data feeds). - Vulnerability assessments, Red Team reports, or other reports from analyses of information systems, subsystems, information technology products, devices, networks, or applications. - Contingency Plans, Disaster Recovery Plans, Incident Reports. - Vendor/manufacturer vulnerability reports.	Yes Via RAR	Yes Via RAR	Yes Via Peer Sharing

---

[55] The term *likelihood*, as discussed in this guideline, is not likelihood in the strict sense of the term; rather, it is a likelihood score. Risk assessors do not define a likelihood function in the statistical sense. Instead, risk assessors assign a score (or likelihood assessment) based on available evidence, experience, and expert judgment. Combinations of factors such as targeting, intent, and capability thus can be used to produce a score representing the likelihood of threat initiation; combinations of factors such as capability and vulnerability severity can be used to produce a score representing the likelihood of adverse impacts; and combinations of these scores can be used to produce an overall likelihood score.

TABLE G-2: ASSESSMENT SCALE – LIKELIHOOD OF THREAT EVENT INITIATION (ADVERSARIAL)

Qualitative Values	Semi-Quantitative Values		Description
Very High	96-100	10	Adversary is **almost certain** to initiate the threat event.
High	80-95	8	Adversary is **highly likely** to initiate the threat event.
Moderate	21-79	5	Adversary is **somewhat likely** to initiate the treat event.
Low	5-20	2	Adversary is **unlikely** to initiate the threat event.
Very Low	0-4	0	Adversary is **highly unlikely** to initiate the threat event.

TABLE G-3: ASSESSMENT SCALE – LIKELIHOOD OF THREAT EVENT OCCURRENCE (NON-ADVERSARIAL)

Qualitative Values	Semi-Quantitative Values		Description
Very High	96-100	10	Error, accident, or act of nature is **almost certain** to occur; or occurs **more than 100 times a year.**
High	80-95	8	Error, accident, or act of nature is **highly likely** to occur; or occurs **between 10-100 times a year.**
Moderate	21-79	5	Error, accident, or act of nature is **somewhat likely** to occur; or occurs **between 1-10 times a year.**
Low	5-20	2	Error, accident, or act of nature is **unlikely** to occur; or occurs **less than once a year**, but **more than once every 10 years.**
Very Low	0-4	0	Error, accident, or act of nature is **highly unlikely** to occur; or occurs **less than once every 10 years.**

TABLE G-4: ASSESSMENT SCALE – LIKELIHOOD OF THREAT EVENT RESULTING IN ADVERSE IMPACTS

Qualitative Values	Semi-Quantitative Values		Description
Very High	96-100	10	If the threat event is initiated or occurs, it is **almost certain** to have adverse impacts.
High	80-95	8	If the threat event is initiated or occurs, it is **highly likely** to have adverse impacts.
Moderate	21-79	5	If the threat event is initiated or occurs, it is **somewhat likely** to have adverse impacts.
Low	5-20	2	If the threat event is initiated or occurs, it is **unlikely** to have adverse impacts.
Very Low	0-4	0	If the threat event is initiated or occurs, it is **highly unlikely** to have adverse impacts.

TABLE G-5: ASSESSMENT SCALE – OVERALL LIKELIHOOD

Likelihood of Threat Event Initiation or Occurrence	Likelihood Threat Events Result in Adverse Impacts				
	Very Low	Low	Moderate	High	Very High
Very High	Low	Moderate	High	Very High	Very High
High	Low	Moderate	Moderate	High	Very High
Moderate	Low	Low	Moderate	Moderate	High
Low	Very Low	Low	Low	Moderate	Moderate
Very Low	Very Low	Very Low	Low	Low	Low

APPENDIX H

IMPACT

EFFECTS OF THREAT EVENTS ON ORGANIZATIONS, INDIVIDUALS, AND THE NATION

This appendix provides: (i) a description of useful inputs to the impact determination task; (ii) representative examples of adverse impacts to organizational operations and assets, individuals, other organizations, or the Nation; (iii) exemplary assessment scales for assessing the impact of threat events and the range of effect of threat events; and (iv) a template for summarizing and documenting the results of the impact determination Task 2-5. The assessment scales in this appendix can be used as a starting point with appropriate tailoring to adjust for any organization-specific conditions. Table H-4, an output from Task 2-5, provides relevant inputs to the risk tables in Appendix I.

TABLE H-1: INPUTS – DETERMINATION OF IMPACT

Description	Provided To		
	Tier 1	Tier 2	Tier 3
From Tier 1 (Organization level) - Impact information and guidance specific to Tier 1 (e.g., impact information related to organizational governance, core missions/business functions, management and operational policies, procedures, and structures, external mission/business relationships). - Guidance on organization-wide levels of impact needing no further consideration. - Identification of critical missions/business functions. - Exemplary set of impacts, annotated by the organization, if necessary. (**Table H-2**) - Assessment scale for assessing the impact of threat events, annotated by the organization, if necessary. (**Table H-3**)	No	Yes	Yes If not provided by Tier 2
From Tier 2: (Mission/business process level) - Impact information and guidance specific to Tier 2 (e.g., impact information related to mission/business processes, EA segments, common infrastructure, support services, common controls, and external dependencies). - Identification of high-value assets.	Yes Via RAR	Yes Via Peer Sharing	Yes
From Tier 3: (Information system level) - Impact information and guidance specific to Tier 3 (e.g., likelihood information affecting information systems, information technologies, information system components, applications, networks, environments of operation). - Historical data on successful and unsuccessful cyber attacks; attack detection rates. - Security assessment reports (i.e., deficiencies in assessed controls identified as vulnerabilities). - Results of continuous monitoring activities (e.g., automated and nonautomated data feeds). - Vulnerability assessments, Red Team reports, or other reports from analyses of information systems, subsystems, information technology products, devices, networks, or applications. - Contingency Plans, Disaster Recovery Plans, Incident Reports.	Yes Via RAR	Yes Via RAR	Yes Via Peer Sharing

TABLE H-2: EXAMPLES OF ADVERSE IMPACTS

Type of Impact	Impact

HARM TO OPERATIONS	- Inability to perform current missions/business functions.
	  - In a sufficiently timely manner.
	  - With sufficient confidence and/or correctness.
	  - Within planned resource constraints.
	- Inability, or limited ability, to perform missions/business functions in the future.
	  - Inability to restore missions/business functions.
	  - In a sufficiently timely manner.
	  - With sufficient confidence and/or correctness.
	  - Within planned resource constraints.
	- Harms (e.g., financial costs, sanctions) due to noncompliance.
	  - With applicable laws or regulations.
	  - With contractual requirements or other requirements in other binding agreements (e.g., liability).
	- Direct financial costs.
	- Relational harms.
	  - Damage to trust relationships.
	  - Damage to image or reputation (and hence future or potential trust relationships).

HARM TO ASSETS	- Damage to or loss of physical facilities. - Damage to or loss of information systems or networks. - Damage to or loss of information technology or equipment. - Damage to or loss of component parts or supplies. - Damage to or of loss of information assets. - Loss of intellectual property.
HARM TO INDIVIDUALS	- Injury or loss of life. - Physical or psychological mistreatment. - Identity theft. - Loss of Personally Identifiable Information. - Damage to image or reputation.

HARM TO OTHER ORGANIZATIONS	- Harms (e.g., financial costs, sanctions) due to noncompliance.
	  - With applicable laws or regulations.
	  - With contractual requirements or other requirements in other binding agreements.
	- Direct financial costs.
	- Relational harms.
	  - Damage to trust relationships.
	  - Damage to reputation (and hence future or potential trust relationships).

HARM TO THE NATION	- Damage to or incapacitation of a critical infrastructure sector.
	- Loss of government continuity of operations.
	- Relational harms.
	  - Damage to trust relationships with other governments or with nongovernmental entities.
	  - Damage to national reputation (and hence future or potential trust relationships).
	- Damage to current or future ability to achieve national objectives.
	  - Harm to national security.

TABLE H-3: ASSESSMENT SCALE – IMPACT OF THREAT EVENTS

Qualitative Values	Semi-Quantitative Values		Description
Very High	96-100	10	The threat event could be expected to have **multiple severe or catastrophic** adverse effects on organizational operations, organizational assets, individuals, other organizations, or the Nation.
High	80-95	8	The threat event could be expected to have a **severe or catastrophic** adverse effect on organizational operations, organizational assets, individuals, other organizations, or the Nation. A severe or catastrophic adverse effect means that, for example, the threat event might: (i) cause a severe degradation in or loss of mission capability to an extent and duration that the organization is not able to perform one or more of its primary functions; (ii) result in major damage to organizational assets; (iii) result in major financial loss; or (iv) result in severe or catastrophic harm to individuals involving loss of life or serious life-threatening injuries.
Moderate	21-79	5	The threat event could be expected to have a **serious** adverse effect on organizational operations, organizational assets, individuals other organizations, or the Nation. A serious adverse effect means that, for example, the threat event might: (i) cause a significant degradation in mission capability to an extent and duration that the organization is able to perform its primary functions, but the effectiveness of the functions is significantly reduced; (ii) result in significant damage to organizational assets; (iii) result in significant financial loss; or (iv) result in significant harm to individuals that does not involve loss of life or serious life-threatening injuries.
Low	5-20	2	The threat event could be expected to have a **limited** adverse effect on organizational operations, organizational assets, individuals other organizations, or the Nation. A limited adverse effect means that, for example, the threat event might: (i) cause a degradation in mission capability to an extent and duration that the organization is able to perform its primary functions, but the effectiveness of the functions is noticeably reduced; (ii) result in minor damage to organizational assets; (iii) result in minor financial loss; or (iv) result in minor harm to individuals.
Very Low	0-4	0	The threat event could be expected to have a **negligible** adverse effect on organizational operations, organizational assets, individuals other organizations, or the Nation.

TABLE H-4: TEMPLATE – IDENTIFICATION OF ADVERSE IMPACTS

Type of Impact	Impact Affected Asset	Maximum Impact
Table H-2 or Organization-defined	Table H-2 or Organization-defined	Table H-3 or Organization-defined

APPENDIX I

RISK DETERMINATION
ASSESSING RISK TO ORGANIZATIONS, INDIVIDUALS, AND THE NATION

T his appendix provides: (i) a description of potentially useful inputs to the risk determination task including considerations for uncertainty of determinations; (ii) exemplary assessment scales for assessing the levels of risk; (iii) tables for describing content (i.e., data inputs) for adversarial and non-adversarial risk determinations; and (iv) templates for summarizing and documenting the results of the risk determination Task 2-6. The assessment scales in this appendix can be used as a starting point with appropriate tailoring to adjust for any organization-specific conditions. Table I-5 (adversarial risk) and Table I-7 (non-adversarial risk) are outputs from Task 2-6.

TABLE I-1: INPUTS – RISK

Description	Provided To		
	Tier 1	Tier 2	Tier 3
From Tier 1 (Organization level) - Sources of risk and uncertainty information identified for organization-wide use (e.g., specific information that may be useful in determining likelihoods such as adversary capabilities, intent, and targeting objectives). - Guidance on organization-wide levels of risk (including uncertainty) needing no further consideration. - Criteria for uncertainty determinations. - List of high-risk events from previous risk assessments. - Assessment scale for assessing the level of risk as a combination of likelihood and impact, annotated by the organization, if necessary. **(Table I-2)** - Assessment scale for assessing level of risk, annotated by the organization, if necessary. **(Table I-3)**	No	Yes	Yes If not provided by Tier 2
From Tier 2: (Mission/business process level) - Risk-related information and guidance specific to Tier 2 (e.g., risk and uncertainty information related to mission/business processes, EA segments, common infrastructure, support services, common controls, and external dependencies).	Yes Via RAR	Yes Via Peer Sharing	Yes
From Tier 3: (Information system level) - Risk-related information and guidance specific to Tier 3 (e.g., likelihood information affecting information systems, information technologies, information system components, applications, networks, environments of operation).	Yes Via RAR	Yes Via RAR	Yes Via Peer Sharing

TABLE I-2: ASSESSMENT SCALE – LEVEL OF RISK (COMBINATION OF LIKELIHOOD AND IMPACT)

Likelihood (Threat Event Occurs and Results in Adverse Impact)	Level of Impact				
	Very Low	**Low**	**Moderate**	**High**	**Very High**
Very High	Very Low	Low	Moderate	High	Very High
High	Very Low	Low	Moderate	High	Very High
Moderate	Very Low	Low	Moderate	Moderate	High
Low	Very Low	Low	Low	Low	Moderate
Very Low	Very Low	Very Low	Very Low	Low	Low

TABLE I-3: ASSESSMENT SCALE – LEVEL OF RISK

Qualitative Values	Semi-Quantitative Values		Description
Very High	96-100	10	**Very high risk** means that a threat event could be expected to have **multiple severe or catastrophic** adverse effects on organizational operations, organizational assets, individuals, other organizations, or the Nation.
High	80-95	8	**High risk** means that a threat event could be expected to have a **severe or catastrophic** adverse effect on organizational operations, organizational assets, individuals, other organizations, or the Nation.
Moderate	21-79	5	**Moderate risk** means that a threat event could be expected to have a **serious** adverse effect on organizational operations, organizational assets, individuals, other organizations, or the Nation.
Low	5-20	2	**Low risk** means that a threat event could be expected to have a **limited** adverse effect on organizational operations, organizational assets, individuals, other organizations, or the Nation.
Very Low	0-4	0	**Very low risk** means that a threat event could be expected to have a **negligible** adverse effect on organizational operations, organizational assets, individuals, other organizations, or the Nation.

TABLE I-4: COLUMN DESCRIPTIONS FOR ADVERSARIAL RISK TABLE

Column	Heading	Content
1	Threat Event	Identify threat event. (Task 2-2; Table E-1; Table E-2; Table E-5; Table I-5.)
2	Threat Sources	Identify threat sources that could initiate the threat event. (Task 2-1; Table D-1; Table D-2; Table D-7; Table I-5.)
3	Capability	Assess threat source capability. (Task 2-1; Table D-3; Table D-7; Table I-5.)
4	Intent	Assess threat source intent. (Task 2-1; Table D-4; Table D-7; Table I-5.)
5	Targeting	Assess threat source targeting. (Task 2-1; Table D-5; Table D-7; Table I-5.)
6	Relevance	Determine relevance of threat event. (Task 2-2; Table E-1; Table E-4; Table E-5; Table I-5.) If the relevance of the threat event does not meet the organization's criteria for further consideration, do not complete the remaining columns.
7	Likelihood of Attack Initiation	Determine likelihood that one or more of the threat sources initiates the threat event, taking into consideration capability, intent, and targeting. (Task 2-4; Table G-1; Table G-2; Table I-5.)
8	Vulnerabilities and Predisposing Conditions	Identify vulnerabilities which could be exploited by threat sources initiating the threat event and the predisposing conditions which could increase the likelihood of adverse impacts. (Task 2-5; Table F-1; Table F-3; Table F-4; Table F-6; Table I-5.)
9	Severity Pervasiveness	Assess severity of vulnerabilities and pervasiveness of predisposing conditions. (Task 2-5; Table F-1; Table F-2; Table F-5; Table F-6; Table I-5.)
10	Likelihood Initiated Attack Succeeds	Determine the likelihood that the threat event, once initiated, will result in adverse impact, taking into consideration threat source capability, vulnerabilities, and predisposing conditions. (Task 2-4; Table G-1; Table G-4; Table I-5.)
11	Overall Likelihood	Determine the likelihood that the threat event will be initiated and result in adverse impact (i.e., combination of likelihood of attack initiation and likelihood that initiated attack succeeds). (Task 2-4; Table G-1; Table G-5; Table I-5.)
12	Level of Impact	Determine the adverse impact (i.e., potential harm to organizational operations, organizational assets, individuals, other organizations, or the Nation) from the threat event. (Task 2-5; Table H-1, Table H-2; Table H-3; Table H-4; Table I-5.)
13	Risk	Determine the level of risk as a combination of likelihood and impact. (Task 2-6; Table I-1; Table I-2; Table I-3; Table I-5.)

TABLE I-5: TEMPLATE – ADVERSARIAL RISK

1	2	3	4	5	6	7	8	9	10	11	12	13
Threat Event	Threat Sources	Threat Source Characteristics			Relevance	Likelihood of Attack Initiation	Vulnerabilities and Predisposing Conditions	Severity and Pervasiveness	Likelihood Initiated Attack Succeeds	Overall Likelihood	Level of Impact	Risk
		Capability	Intent	Targeting								

TABLE I-6: COLUMN DESCRIPTIONS FOR NON-ADVERSARIAL RISK TABLE

Column	Heading	Content
1	Threat Event	Identify threat event. (**Task 2-2; Table E-1; Table E-3; Table E-5; Table I-7.**)
2	Threat Sources	Identify threat sources that could initiate the threat event. (**Task 2-1; Table D-1; Table D-2; Table D-8; Table I-7.**)
3	Range of Effects	Identify the range of effects from the threat source. (**Task 2-1; Table D-1; Table D-6; Table I-7.**)
4	Relevance	Determine relevance of threat event. (**Task 2-2; Table E-1; Table E-4; Table E-5; Table I-7.**) If the relevance of the threat event does not meet the organization's criteria for further consideration, do not complete the remaining columns.
5	Likelihood of Threat Event Occurring	Determine the likelihood that the threat event will occur. (**Task 2-4; Table G-1; Table G-3; Table I-7.**)
6	Vulnerabilities and Predisposing Conditions	Identify vulnerabilities which could be exploited by threat sources initiating the threat event and the predisposing conditions which could increase the likelihood of adverse impacts. (**Task 2-5; Table F-1; Table F-3; Table F-4; Table F-6; Table I-7.**)
7	Severity Pervasiveness	Assess severity of vulnerabilities and pervasiveness of predisposing conditions. (**Task 2-5; Table F-1; Table F-2; Table F-5; Table F-6; Table I-5.**)
8	Likelihood Threat Event Results in Adverse Impact	Determine the likelihood that the threat event, once initiated, will result in adverse impact, taking into consideration vulnerabilities and predisposing conditions. (**Task 2-4; Table G-1; Table G-4; Table I-7.**)
9	Overall Likelihood	Determine the likelihood that the threat event will occur and result in adverse impacts (i.e., combination of likelihood of threat occurring and likelihood that the threat event results in adverse impact). (**Task 2-4; Table G-1; Table G-5; Table I-7.**)
10	Level of Impact	Determine the adverse impact (i.e., potential harm to organizational operations, organizational assets, individuals, other organizations, or the Nation) from the threat event. (**Task 2-5; Table H-1, Table H-2; Table H-3; Table H-4; Table I-7.**)
11	Risk	Determine the level of risk as a combination of likelihood and impact. (**Task 2-6; Table I-1; Table I-2; Table I-3; Table I-7.**)

TABLE I-7: TEMPLATE – NON-ADVERSARIAL RISK

1	2	3	4	5	6	7	8	9	10	11
Threat Event	Threat Sources	Range of Effects	Relevance	Likelihood of Event Occurring	Vulnerabilities and Predisposing Conditions	Severity and Pervasiveness	Likelihood Event Results in Adverse Impact	Overall Likelihood	Level of Impact	Risk

APPENDIX J

INFORMING RISK RESPONSE

APPROACHES TO REFINING RISK ASSESSMENT RESULTS

A risk assessment may identify a number of risks that have similar scores (e.g., 78, 82, 83) or levels (e.g., moderate, high). When too many risks are clustered at or about the same value, organizations need a method to refine the presentation of risk assessment results, prioritizing within sets of risks with similar values, to better inform the risk response component of the risk management process.[56] Such a method should be associated with the mission/business requirements of the organization, consistent with the organizational risk tolerance, and maximize the use of available resources. Prioritization is a key component of risk-based protection and becomes necessary when requirements cannot be fully satisfied or when resources do not allow all risks to be mitigated within a reasonable time frame. To facilitate informed risk response decisions by senior leaders/executives (e.g., why certain risks were or were not mitigated), the risk assessment results are annotated to enable those decision makers to know or obtain the answers to the following questions about each risk in a set with similar scores:

Time Frame

In the event the identified risk materialized—

- How high would the *immediate* impact be to organizational operations (including mission, functions, image, or reputation), organizational assets, individuals, other organizations, or the Nation?

- How high would the *future* impact be to organizational operations (including mission, functions, image, or reputation), organizational assets, individuals, other organizations, or the Nation?

The answers to the above questions, together with the risk tolerance of the organization, provide the basis for a risk prioritization that is based on current and future organizational needs. When weighing immediate impacts versus future impacts, senior leaders must decide whether a critical mission/business need today warrants jeopardizing the future capabilities of the organization. Mission/business owners and mission/business subject matter experts can be consulted to obtain the most complete and up-to-date information on mission/business impacts. Other subject matter experts or stakeholder representatives can be consulted to obtain information on immediate versus future impacts (e.g., consulting the Privacy Office for impacts to individuals).

Total Cumulative Impact

- What is the expected impact from a single occurrence of the threat?

- If the risk can materialize more than once, what is the overall expected impact (i.e., cumulative loss) for the time period of concern?

Note that one aspect of the total impact to organizations is the cost of recovery from a loss of confidentiality, integrity, or availability.

---

[56] The *risk executive (function)* provides policy-level guidance on organizational risk tolerance and other factors that inform and guide the risk-based decisions of authorizing officials. This guidance can also influence the prioritization of risk responses including for example, mitigation activities.

Synergies Among Risks

If a risk materializes that is closely related to multiple risks, it is likely that a cluster of risks will materialize at or near the same time. Managing the adverse impact from one risk materializing may be possible; managing multiple risks of high impact that materialize at the same time may challenge the capacity of the organization and therefore needs to be managed much more closely. The following questions address relationships among risks.

Will the materialization of a particular risk result in:

- A high likelihood or virtual certainty of other identified risks materializing?

- A high likelihood or virtual certainty of other identified risks *not* materializing?

- No particular effect on other identified risks materializing?

If a risk is highly coupled to other risks or seen as likely to lead to other risks materializing (whether the risk is the cause or materializes concurrently), the risk should be given higher priority than a risk that has no particular effect on other risks. If a risk materializing actually decreases the likelihood of other risks materializing, then further analysis is warranted to determine which risks become a lower priority to mitigate.

In conclusion, organizations can benefit significantly by refining risk assessment results in preparation for the risk response step in the risk management process. During the risk response step, which is described in NIST Special Publication 800-39, organizations: (i) analyze different courses of action; (ii) conduct cost-benefit analyses; (iii) address scalability issues for large-scale implementations; (iv) examine the interactions/dependencies among risk mitigation approaches (e.g., dependencies among security controls); and (v) assess other factors affecting organizational missions/business functions. In addition, organizations address cost, schedule, and performance issues associated with information systems and information technology infrastructure supporting organizational missions/business functions.

CAUTIONARY NOTE

Organizations are cautioned that risk assessments are often not precise instruments of measurement and reflect the limitations of the specific assessment methodologies, tools, and techniques employed—as well as the subjectivity, quality, and trustworthiness of the data used. Risk determinations may be very coarse due to the assessment approach selected, the uncertainty in the likelihood of occurrence and impact values, and the potential mischaracterization of threats. Risks that are on the borderline between bins using the organization-defined binning scales, must ultimately be assigned to one bin. This determination could have a significant effect on the risk prioritization process. Thus, organizations should incorporate as much information as practical on particular risks during the prioritization process to ensure that the values for risks are appropriately determined (e.g., very low, low, moderate, high, very high).

APPENDIX K

RISK ASSESSMENT REPORTS
ESSENTIAL ELEMENTS OF INFORMATION

This appendix provides the essential elements of information that organizations can use to communicate the results of risk assessments.[57] Risk assessment results provide decision makers with an understanding of the information security risk to organizational operations and assets, individuals, other organizations, or the Nation that derive from the operation and use of organizational information systems and the environments in which those systems operate. The essential elements of information in a risk assessment can be described in three sections of the risk assessment report (or whatever vehicle is chosen by organizations to convey the results of the assessment): (i) an executive summary; (ii) the main body containing detailed risk assessment results; and (iii) supporting appendices.

Executive Summary

- List the date of the risk assessment.

- Summarize the purpose of the risk assessment.

- Describe the scope of the risk assessment.

  - For Tier 1 and Tier 2 risk assessments, identify: organizational governance structures or processes associated with the assessment (e.g., risk executive [function], budget process, acquisition process, systems engineering process, enterprise architecture, information security architecture, organizational missions/business functions, mission/business processes, information systems supporting the mission/business processes).

  - For Tier 3 risk assessments, identify: the information system name and location(s), security categorization, and information system (i.e., authorization) boundary.

- State whether this is an initial or subsequent risk assessment. If a subsequent risk assessment, state the circumstances that prompted the update and include a reference to the previous Risk Assessment Report.

- Describe the overall level of risk (e.g., Very Low, Low, Moderate, High, or Very High).

- List the number of risks identified for each level of risk (e.g., Very Low, Low, Moderate, High, or Very High).

Body of the Report

- Describe the purpose of the risk assessment, including questions to be answered by the assessment. For example:

---

[57] The essential elements of information described in this appendix are informative and exemplary only and are not intended to require or promote a specific template for documenting risk assessment results. Organizations have maximum flexibility in determining the type and the level of detail of information included in organizational risk assessments and the associated reports. For example, Tier 1 and Tier 2 risk assessment results may be conveyed via an executive briefing or dashboard, whereas Tier 3 risk assessment results may be conveyed via a risk assessment report (formal or informal depending on organizational preference). The essential elements of information for communicating risk assessment results can be modified accordingly to meet the needs of organizations conducting the assessments.

- How the use of a specific information technology would potentially change the risk to organizational missions/business functions if employed in information systems supporting those missions/business functions; or

- How the risk assessment results are to be used in the context of the RMF (e.g., an initial risk assessment to be used in tailoring security control baselines and/or to guide and inform other decisions and serve as a starting point for subsequent risk assessments; subsequent risk assessment to incorporate results of security control assessments and inform authorization decisions; subsequent risk assessment to support the analysis of alternative courses of action for risk responses; subsequent risk assessment based on risk monitoring to identify new threats or vulnerabilities; subsequent risk assessments to incorporate knowledge gained from incidents or attacks).

- Identify assumptions and constraints.

- Describe risk tolerance inputs to the risk assessment (including the range of consequences to be considered).

- Identify and describe the risk model and analytic approach; provide a reference or include as an appendix, identifying risk factors, value scales, and algorithms for combining values.

- Provide a rationale for any risk-related decisions during the risk assessment process.

- Describe the uncertainties within the risk assessment process and how those uncertainties influence decisions.

- If the risk assessment includes organizational missions/business functions, describe the missions/functions (e.g., mission/business processes supporting the missions/functions, interconnections and dependencies among related missions/business functions, and information technology that supports the missions/business functions).

- If the risk assessment includes organizational information systems, describe the systems (e.g., missions/business functions the system is supporting, information flows to/from the systems, and dependencies on other systems, shared services, or common infrastructures).

- Summarize risk assessment results (e.g., using tables or graphs), in a form that enables decision makers to quickly understand the risk (e.g., number of threat events for different combinations of likelihood and impact, the relative proportion of threat events at different risk levels).

- Identify the time frame for which the risk assessment is valid (i.e., time frame for which the assessment is intended to support decisions).

- List the risks due to adversarial threats (see Table F-1).

- List the risks due to non-adversarial threats (see Table F-2).

Appendices

- List references and sources of information.

- List the team or individuals conducting the risk assessment including contact information.

- List risk assessment details and any supporting evidence (e.g., Tables D-7, D-8, E-5, F-3, F-6, H-4), as needed to understand and enable reuse of results (e.g., for reciprocity, for subsequent risk assessments, to serve as input to Tier 1 and Tier 2 risk assessments).

APPENDIX L

SUMMARY OF TASKS
RISK ASSESSMENT TASKS AND ASSOCIATED RISK TABLES

TABLE L-1: SUMMARY OF RISK ASSESSMENT TASKS

TASK	TASK DESCRIPTION
Step 1: Prepare for Risk Assessment	
TASK 1-1 IDENTIFY PURPOSE Section 3.1	Identify the purpose of the risk assessment in terms of the information that the assessment is intended to produce and the decisions the assessment is intended to support.
TASK 1-2 IDENTIFY SCOPE Section 3.1	Identify the scope of the risk assessment in terms of organizational applicability, time frame supported, and architectural/technology considerations.
TASK 1-3 IDENTIFY ASSUMPTIONS AND CONSTRAINTS Section 3.1	Identify the specific assumptions and constraints under which the risk assessment is conducted.
TASK 1-4 IDENTIFY INFORMATION SOURCES Section 3.1	Identify the sources of descriptive, threat, vulnerability, and impact information to be used in the risk assessment.
TASK 1-5 IDENTIFY RISK MODEL AND ANALYTIC APPROACH Section 3.1	Identify the risk model and analytic approach to be used in the risk assessment.
Step 2: Conduct Risk Assessment	
TASK 2-1 IDENTIFY THREAT SOURCES Section 3.2, Appendix D	Identify and characterize threat sources of concern, including capability, intent, and targeting characteristics for adversarial threats and range of effects for non-adversarial threats.
TASK 2-2 IDENTIFY THREAT EVENTS Section 3.2, Appendix E	Identify potential threat events, relevance of the events, and the threat sources that could initiate the events.
TASK 2-3 IDENTIFY VULNERABILITIES AND PREDISPOSING CONDITIONS Section 3.2, Appendix F	Identify vulnerabilities and predisposing conditions that affect the likelihood that threat events of concern result in adverse impacts.

TASK	TASK DESCRIPTION
TASK 2-4 DETERMINE LIKELIHOOD Section 3.2, Appendix G	Determine the likelihood that threat events of concern result in adverse impacts, considering: (i) the characteristics of the threat sources that could initiate the events; (ii) the vulnerabilities/predisposing conditions identified; and (iii) the organizational susceptibility reflecting the safeguards/countermeasures planned or implemented to impede such events.
TASK 2-5 DETERMINE IMPACT Section 3.2, Appendix H	Determine the adverse impacts from threat events of concern, considering: (i) the characteristics of the threat sources that could initiate the events; (ii) the vulnerabilities/predisposing conditions identified; and (iii) the organizational susceptibility reflecting the safeguards/countermeasures planned or implemented to impede such events.
TASK 2-6 DETERMINE RISK Section 3.2, Appendix I	Determine the risk to the organization from threat events of concern considering: (i) the impact that would result from the events; and (ii) the likelihood of the events occurring.
Step 3: Communicate and Share Risk Assessment Results	
TASK 3-1 COMMUNICATE RISK ASSESSMENT RESULTS Section 3.3, Appendix K	Communicate risk assessment results to organizational decision makers to support risk responses.
TASK 3-2 SHARE RISK-RELATED INFORMATION Section 3.3	Share risk-related information produced during the risk assessment with appropriate organizational personnel.
Step 4: Maintain Risk Assessment	
TASK 4-1 MONITOR RISK FACTORS Section 3.4	Conduct ongoing monitoring of the risk factors that contribute to changes in risk to organizational operations and assets, individuals, other organizations, or the Nation.
TASK 4-2 UPDATE RISK ASSESSMENT Section 3.4	Update existing risk assessment using the results from ongoing monitoring of risk factors.

www.ingramcontent.com/pod-product-compliance
Lightning Source LLC
Chambersburg PA
CBHW060452060326
40689CB00020B/4505